# Table of Contents

Title Page

Copyright

Front Matter

Table of Contents

Introduction

Understanding Remote Work

The Evolution of Remote Work

Trends Shaping the Future of Remote Work

Setting Up Your Remote Workspace

Essential Tools for Remote Work

Home Office Design for Maximum Productivity

Technology and Connectivity

Choosing the Right Devices

Ensuring a Reliable Internet Connection

Time Management Strategies

Prioritizing Tasks Effectively

Overcoming Procrastination

Maintaining Work-Life Balance

Creating Boundaries Between Work and Home

Strategies for Disconnecting

Communication in a Remote World

Leveraging Digital Communication Tools

Developing Effective Communication Skills

Collaborative Tools for Remote Teams

Selecting the Best Collaboration Platforms

Optimizing Team Workflow

Building a Remote Work Community

Networking with Other Remote Workers

Participating in Online Communities

Staying Productive on the Go

Adapting to Work While Traveling

Portable Tools and Apps

Managing Remote Teams

Leadership Skills for Virtual Teams

Tracking Progress and Accountability

The Nomadic Lifestyle

Embracing the Freedom of Remote Work

Stories from Successful Digital Nomads

Handling Work Challenges Remotely

Navigating Remote Work Loneliness

Dealing with Technological Issues

Financial Management for Remote Workers

Budgeting for Variable Income

Tax Considerations

Personal Development and Learning

Opportunities for Online Learning

Balancing Skill Development with Work

Remote Work in Different Cultures

Adapting to Cultural Differences

Overcoming Language Barriers

Security and Privacy

Protecting Your Data

Understanding Cybersecurity Basics

The Future of Remote Work

Predicting Industry Changes

The Role of Automation

Health and Well-Being

Maintaining Physical Health

Mental Health Strategies

Creative Professions in a Remote Setting

Opportunities for Artists and Creatives

Collaboration in Creative Fields

Entrepreneurship for the Remote Worker

Starting Your Own Remote Business

Case Studies of Successful Ventures

The Legal Aspects of Remote Work

Understanding Worker Rights

Contract Basics

Navigating Remote Work Policies

Remote Work Agreements

Legal Implications

Remote Work Across Time Zones

Coordinating International Teams

Timing and Scheduling Best Practices

Advancing Your Career Remotely

Promotions and Growth Opportunities

Building a Remote Career Path

Emergency Preparedness for Remote Workers

Contingency Planning

Adapting to Unexpected Changes

Conclusion

Appendix

# The Digital Nomad's Playbook

by

David Holman

Copyright 2024 David Holman. All rights reserved.

No part of this book may be reproduced in any form or by any electronic or mechanical means including information storage and retrieval systems, without permission in writing from the author. The only exception is by a reviewer, who may quote short excerpts in a review.

Although the author and publisher have made every effort to ensure that the information in this book was correct at press time, the author and publisher do not assume and hereby disclaim any liability to any party for any loss, damage, or disruption caused by errors or omissions, whether such errors or omissions result from negligence, accident, or any other cause.

This publication is designed to provide accurate and authoritative information with regard to the subject matter covered. It is sold with the understanding that the publisher is not engaged in rendering professional services. If legal advice or other expert assistance is required, the services of a competent professional should be sought.

The fact that an organization or website is referred to in this work as a citation and/or a potential source of further information does not mean that the author or the publisher endorses the information the organization or website may provide or recommendations it may make.

Please remember that Internet websites listed in this work may have changed or disappeared between when this work was written and when it is read.

The Digital Nomad's Playbook

# Contents

**Introduction**

**Chapter 1: Understanding Remote Work**

    The Evolution of Remote Work

    Trends Shaping the Future of Remote Work

**Chapter 2: Setting Up Your Remote Workspace**

    Essential Tools for Remote Work

    Home Office Design for Maximum Productivity

**Chapter 3: Technology and Connectivity**

    Choosing the Right Devices

    Ensuring a Reliable Internet Connection

**Chapter 4: Time Management Strategies**

    Prioritizing Tasks Effectively

    Overcoming Procrastination

**Chapter 5: Maintaining Work-Life Balance**

    Creating Boundaries Between Work and Home

    Strategies for Disconnecting

**Chapter 6: Communication in a Remote World**

    Leveraging Digital Communication Tools

    Developing Effective Communication Skills

**Chapter 7: Collaborative Tools for Remote Teams**

Selecting the Best Collaboration Platforms

Optimizing Team Workflow

## Chapter 8: Building a Remote Work Community

Networking with Other Remote Workers

Participating in Online Communities

## Chapter 9: Staying Productive on the Go

Adapting to Work While Traveling

Portable Tools and Apps

## Chapter 10: Managing Remote Teams

Leadership Skills for Virtual Teams

Tracking Progress and Accountability

## Chapter 11: The Nomadic Lifestyle

Embracing the Freedom of Remote Work

Stories from Successful Digital Nomads

## Chapter 12: Handling Work Challenges Remotely

Navigating Remote Work Loneliness

Dealing with Technological Issues

## Chapter 13: Financial Management for Remote Workers

Budgeting for Variable Income

Tax Considerations

## Chapter 14: Personal Development and Learning

Opportunities for Online Learning

Balancing Skill Development with Work

## Chapter 15: Remote Work in Different Cultures

Adapting to Cultural Differences

Overcoming Language Barriers

## Chapter 16: Security and Privacy

Protecting Your Data

Understanding Cybersecurity Basics

## Chapter 17: The Future of Remote Work

Predicting Industry Changes

The Role of Automation

## Chapter 18: Health and Well-Being

Maintaining Physical Health

Mental Health Strategies

## Chapter 19: Creative Professions in a Remote Setting

Opportunities for Artists and Creatives

Collaboration in Creative Fields

## Chapter 20: Entrepreneurship for the Remote Worker

Starting Your Own Remote Business

Case Studies of Successful Ventures

## Chapter 21: The Legal Aspects of Remote Work

- Understanding Worker Rights
- Contract Basics

## Chapter 22: Navigating Remote Work Policies

- Remote Work Agreements
- Legal Implications

## Chapter 23: Remote Work Across Time Zones

- Coordinating International Teams
- Timing and Scheduling Best Practices

## Chapter 24: Advancing Your Career Remotely

- Promotions and Growth Opportunities
- Building a Remote Career Path

## Chapter 25: Emergency Preparedness for Remote Workers

- Contingency Planning
- Adapting to Unexpected Changes

## Conclusion

## Appendix A: Appendix

# Introduction

In the ever-evolving landscape of modern work, the concept of a traditional office space is rapidly becoming a relic of the past. As we embrace living in a digital age, more professionals than ever are turning their gaze to the possibilities offered by remote work. This shift isn't just a passing trend; it's a profound transformation that affects people across industries, bringing about new challenges and opportunities. More than simply transplanting office tasks to a home setting, remote work is reshaping how we think about productivity, connectivity, and the balance between personal and professional life.

For many, the allure of remote work is undeniable. The freedom to set your own schedule, the flexibility to work from nearly anywhere, and the possibility to create a customized work environment all contribute to its growing popularity. However, with freedom comes the responsibility to craft a lifestyle and work habits that not only bolster productivity but also nurture personal well-being. This is where our journey begins: to explore the full potential of remote work and equip you to thrive in this new environment.

The advent of remote work raises several questions: How can we establish effective communication when our colleagues are scattered across time zones? What tools and technologies will best support our virtual interactions? How do we maintain a healthy work-life balance when there are no clear boundaries between our office and home? These are just some of the challenges remote workers face and the impetus behind delving into this guide.

Remote work isn't merely about location; it's a mindset. It's about developing the resilience to adapt to new environments and leveraging technology to enhance, rather than hinder, our work. The pages ahead will introduce strategies and insights to help you navigate this landscape, whether you're a seasoned remote worker or just beginning your journey. We'll cover everything from setting up your workspace to managing your time effectively and fostering a sense of community and connection even when miles apart.

Moreover, in a world where the lines between personal and professional spheres are increasingly blurred, maintaining balance becomes crucial. It's not just about keeping up productivity but also ensuring mental and physical health remain priorities. We'll touch on methods to create boundaries and techniques to unwind, ensuring that while you give your best to work, you also reserve the best for yourself.

Adapting to remote work goes beyond simple adjustments in work habits. It requires cultivating relationships without the benefit of physical presence, relying on trust and communication as the glue holding everything together. Understanding how to motivate and lead in a virtual environment is vital, as is learning to collaborate using digital tools designed to bridge physical gaps.

In this rapidly advancing digital age, continuous learning is more accessible than ever, yet we must navigate the vast sea of information intelligently. We must balance the acquisition of new skills with our existing responsibilities. The chapters ahead will provide you with insights into personal development and growth, vital components for anyone seeking to climb the career ladder from a distance.

As remote work continues to redefine professional norms, it's crucial to anticipate future developments. By understanding trends and preparing for potential challenges, both those predictable and unexpected, we'll be better equipped to adapt. This guide aims to not only offer solutions for immediate issues but foster a mindset that embraces change.

This book provides a roadmap to harness the benefits of remote work, circumvent the pitfalls, and emerge successful and fulfilled. Our collective goal is to inspire new ways of thinking, encouraging you to reimagine what's possible in a decentralized work environment. In doing so, we set the stage for a work-life that's not only productive but also enriched with purpose and satisfaction.

As we embark on this exploration, keep an open mind to the possibilities that lie ahead. Remote work isn't merely a means to an end; it's a journey to a flexible, dynamic, and fulfilling career and lifestyle. Let us guide, inspire, and provide the tools needed for you to flourish in this brave new world.

# Chapter 1: Understanding Remote Work

Remote work has leapt from a niche option to a mainstream phenomenon. As organizations and individuals worldwide adapt, the shift toward flexible work environments is more than a simple change of address from office to home. It's a transformation that challenges conventional views on productivity, work-life balance, and the very nature of professional commitment.

For many, remote work represents the freedom to craft a more balanced life, aligning work schedules with personal goals and family responsibilities. The appeal is undeniable—no more long commutes, cumbersome office attire, or rigid clock-in times. This newfound flexibility, however, comes with its own set of challenges, such as isolation and the blurring of lines between professional and personal life. To thrive, one must navigate these potential pitfalls with intention.

Understanding the roots and future trajectories of remote work helps us harness its full potential. Historically, telecommuting has evolved significantly from its beginnings in the 1970s. Today, technological advances and a globalized workforce enable unparalleled connectivity and collaboration across borders. As trends continue to evolve, adaptability becomes the cornerstone of success in remote settings. The future is not just about working remotely, but working smarter and more inclusively in a digital-first world.

To truly grasp the nuances of remote work, we must acknowledge the diverse experiences of individuals in various roles and industries. Every professional's journey is unique, shaped by personal aspirations, organizational culture, and the tools at their disposal. Encouraging a mindset open to change and continuous learning empowers remote workers to succeed and contribute meaningfully to their teams, no matter where they are in the world.

## The Evolution of Remote Work

The concept of remote work isn't as novel as it might seem. Long before the advent of the internet and the digital tools driving today's remote work culture, pioneering figures were exploring the possibility of working away from traditional office spaces. Telecommuting, as it was once called, emerged in the 1970s during an era when rising oil prices and congestion in urban areas led people to consider alternatives to lengthy daily commutes. Back then, technological constraints meant that only a few select individuals could truly benefit from such arrangements, but the idea had been planted.

In the 1980s and 1990s, the personal computer revolution started to open new doors. Companies began to see the potential for distributed work teams, albeit on a modest scale. During this period, remote work was still predominantly confined to tech-savvy roles, and access was generally limited to high-ranking executives or specialized consultants. Physical offices remained the primary locus of business operations, firmly tethering most workers to a specific geographic location.

Then came the internet—a game-changing force that reshaped how we engage with work. The early 2000s gave birth to connectivity improvements that allowed remote work to become more than just a fringe benefit. Broadband internet, email, and cloud computing transformed the landscape, making it feasible for businesses to support remote teams effectively. The initial reluctance from companies eased as they started noticing the potential for increased productivity, reduced costs, and wider talent pools.

Despite the technological readiness, cultural inertia persisted. Many organizations held onto ingrained beliefs about productivity and supervision that tethered employees to the physical office. However, as digital natives entered the workforce, their comfort with virtual communication tools catalyzed a cultural shift towards embracing flexible work arrangements. The so-called "gig economy" further fueled this evolution, prompting a reevaluation of traditional employment models.

The shift, while gradual, gained unexpected momentum with the COVID-19 pandemic. Almost overnight, businesses across the globe found themselves forced to adopt remote work practices to survive. This wasn't just an emergency response; it became a massive, real-world experiment in the viability of remote work at scale. What was once a privilege or an exception suddenly became the norm, accelerating the timeline for organizational change.

As workers and companies settled into this new normal, they discovered a wealth of benefits. Employees experienced the freedom to tailor their work environments—balancing productivity with personal needs. No longer constrained by geography, organizations tapped into broader pools of talent, fostering culturally diverse and dynamic teams. Financial savings emerged as a significant upside, with reduced office space leading to lowered overheads.

This accelerated acceptance introduced new challenges as well. Managers and workers alike had to navigate issues around communication, performance tracking, and team cohesion in this decentralized setup. However, the potential for innovation often lies within the adjustments and adaptations made in response to such challenges.

Technological advancements continue to shape and redefine what remote work looks like. Video conferencing tools, project management software, and enhanced cybersecurity measures are just a few pieces of the continuously evolving puzzle, making remote work more efficient and secure. We now find ourselves at a fascinating juncture, where even traditional industries are rethinking their positions on work location flexibility.

The evolution of remote work doesn't merely stop at logistical improvements and technological advancements. It emphasizes a change in mindset—a shift towards recognizing output over hours, valuing autonomy, and trusting employees to manage their responsibilities effectively. The burgeoning popularity of asynchronous work further emphasizes this point, presenting opportunities for people to manage their time more flexibly while contributing meaningfully to their roles.

It's clear the future of work is not a return to the "business as usual" of the past. Remote work, whether hybrid or fully distributed, is poised to be a significant aspect of professional life going forward. Companies are increasingly seeing remote work not as a stopgap but as a strategic advantage that aligns with broader goals of sustainability, equity, and globalization.

Understanding the evolution of remote work helps us appreciate the path to where we are today. It frames the context in which remote workers and managers operate, equipping them to face current and future challenges with resilience and creativity. As the landscape continues to evolve, it's not just about adapting to change but also embracing the opportunities that come with this transformative way of working.

## Trends Shaping the Future of Remote Work

The landscape of remote work is evolving faster than ever, influenced by technological advancements, shifting workforce expectations, and global events. At the heart of these changes is the unprecedented flexibility now available to workers, reshaping how, where, and when work gets done. The remote work trends emerging now are not only shaping the present but are pivotal in defining the future of work itself.

One of the most significant drivers of remote work trends is technology. From virtual reality meetings to AI-driven project management tools, technology is both a catalyst and a facilitator. It is enhancing connectivity, allowing teams to collaborate in ways previously unimaginable. The reliance on digital tools—think Slack for communication, Asana for task management, or Zoom for video calls—has become second nature. As these tools evolve, they continue to reduce the physical barriers, making remote work more seamless and integrated.

AI and machine learning are starting to play a more central role in remote work settings. These technologies are being used not just for automating mundane tasks but for enhancing decision-making processes and personalizing work experiences. They help sift through massive amounts of data to generate insights, offering a competitive edge to freelancers and organizations alike.

The shift towards a more distributed workforce means that companies are no longer constrained by geography when seeking talent. For workers, it means access to global opportunities without the necessity of relocation. This freedom opens doors to diverse experiences and perspectives, enriching workplaces across the board. It allows employees to work from locales where they are happiest and most productive, driving satisfaction and retention.

- **Hybrid Work Models:** The hybrid work model is gaining traction and it's clear why. Combining remote and in-office work offers the best of both worlds, enhancing flexibility while maintaining physical workspace for collaboration and face-to-face interactions.

- **Focus on Well-Being:** As remote work trends evolve, there's a growing emphasis on employee well-being. Companies are increasingly aware that ensuring the mental and physical health of their workforce is key to maintaining productivity and job satisfaction.

- **Specialized Remote Tools:** Credit must be given to the explosion of tools built specifically for remote work. From facilitating asynchronous communication to providing a platform for virtual team-building activities, these tools cater to every need that arises from a decentralized workforce.

The demographic shift can't be ignored either. Millennials and Gen Z are now a substantial part of the workforce. They prioritize flexibility and purpose over traditional workplace motivators. Their values drive companies to rethink work culture, making it more inclusive and balanced. They view remote work as the norm rather than a perk, anchoring their expectations in a fluid job market.

Additionally, the pandemic has reshaped how we approach work. What was once seen as a temporary shift to working from home has solidified into a permanent preference for many. Businesses have adapted, and many have discovered the logistical and cost benefits of cutting down on office space and eliminating long commutes. This global event forced organizations worldwide to rethink and reenact their strategies surrounding remote work, bringing to fore more flexible options for employees.

Remote work policies and practices are being institutionalized. Progressive organizations are crafting comprehensive remote-first policies to ensure equity and effectiveness, listening to employee feedback to fine-tune these policies. Likewise, remote onboarding practices are evolving, fostering inclusivity and bringing a sense of belonging even when new hires are miles away from their teams.

There is also an increased emphasis on continuous learning and upskilling. As industries face rapid technological evolution, the need to adapt and learn new skills is more relevant than ever. Companies understand this necessity and are investing in training programs, supporting their workforce's growth irrespective of geographical location, feeding into a culture of lifelong learning.

But with these trends come new challenges. Cybersecurity is a major concern, particularly given the dispersed nature of remote teams. As workers access networks from a variety of locations, ensuring the protection of sensitive data demands robust strategies and constant vigilance.

Moreover, the transition to remote work spurs discussion on employee monitoring and trust. While some businesses consider monitoring software, others focus on fostering a culture of trust and autonomy. The balance between oversight and freedom is delicate but essential for nurturing productive work environments.

There's a social element to consider as well. The rise of remote work is changing city landscapes and cultures. Urban centers traditionally known for career opportunities are adapting as workers disperse to suburban, rural, or even exotic locations, profoundly impacting the socio-economic fabric of these regions.

Ultimately, the trends shaping the future of remote work are diverse and multifaceted. They reflect broader cultural and technological shifts, urging both individuals and organizations to adapt, innovate, and rethink traditional work structures. As these trends continue to unfold, they will redefine not just how we work, but how we view work in relation to life, society, and personal fulfillment.

# Chapter 2: Setting Up Your Remote Workspace

Creating an ideal remote workspace isn't just about squeezing a desk into a corner of your living room; it's about crafting a zone where productivity and creativity thrive. Your workspace is your command center, a direct reflection of how you function daily. Invest the time to tailor this environment—a place where your mind can focus, distractions fade away, and your best work comes to life.

Start by assessing the tools you need. Whether it's a dual-monitor setup for enhanced multitasking or noise-canceling headphones to block out background noise, the right equipment can transform your work experience. Think of ergonomics; a comfortable chair and desk height can prevent those nagging aches and pains that come from hours of sitting. Setting up an effective workspace is not just about immediate ease but also about sustainable practices that support your well-being over time.

Your workspace should be a haven for productivity, but aesthetics matter too. Visual elements, like color and lighting, affect mood significantly. Consider the use of natural light or lamps that mimic daylight to keep your energy levels high. Personal touches, such as a plant or artwork, can make the environment inviting, fostering a positive mindset and boosting motivation. After all, a space that feels good encourages better work.

Finally, test your setup ergonomically and technologically. Make adjustments until you find the perfect balance between comfort and utility. As you work, you'll notice which aspects help or hinder your focus, allowing for continuous improvements. Embrace this dynamic process and allow your workspace to evolve with you. A well-crafted remote workspace isn't just a backdrop to your work—it is a central part of your professional success.

## Essential Tools for Remote Work

Imagine waking up each morning with the opportunity to mold your workspace into a haven of productivity. That's one of the perks of remote work—crafting an environment that works for you. But to truly elevate your remote work setup, a selection of essential tools is indispensable. These tools not only enhance productivity but also shape how we engage and connect in a decentralized work environment.

At the heart of any remote work toolkit is a reliable computer or laptop. This device serves as your primary portal into the digital landscape where your work unfolds. Choose one that aligns with your professional needs—whether it's a powerful machine for graphic design or a laptop with long battery life for video conferencing. Remember, the agility and performance of your device can dramatically shape your work experience, so prioritize reliability and capability.

Next on the list is a dependable internet connection. It might seem obvious, but your internet is your lifeline to the world beyond your home office. It's worth investing in a robust plan and perhaps a backup solution, like a mobile hotspot, to avoid being at the mercy of unpredictable outages. The stability of your connection can make or break your ability to participate in remote meetings and collaborate with colleagues far and wide.

Communication is key in remote work. Tools like Slack, Microsoft Teams, or Zoom facilitate smooth interactions with team members, bridging the gaps often present in digital communications. These platforms support chat functionalities, video calls, and even file sharing, enabling seamless teamwork and collaboration. Try different tools to see which best fits your team dynamics and workflows.

Project management tools make up another critical component of your remote arsenal. Applications like Asana, Trello, or Monday.com offer frameworks for organizing tasks, setting deadlines, and tracking progress. By instituting a sense of structure, these tools ensure that projects remain on track and that everyone knows their responsibilities and timelines.

Cloud storage solutions like Google Drive, Dropbox, or OneDrive allow for safe, secure sharing and access to your important files. With these, you can achieve that balance of accessibility and security, enabling you and your team to work effectively from anywhere, at any time.

Noise-canceling headphones can be a game-changer. They create a bubble of concentration, shielding you from distractions whether you're working from a bustling café or a lively household. These headphones help maintain focus during video calls, ensuring that background noise doesn't interfere with important conversations.

Along with audible focus, visual clarity matters—so invest in a good webcam and microphone if they aren't already top-notch on your device. Crystal-clear video and audio make a difference in remote meetings, building a professional image and fostering better connections with coworkers who rely on non-verbal cues.

Beyond these core tools, there are several productivity enhancements that can amplify your effectiveness. Utilizing multiple monitors, for instance, provides expansive digital real estate, making multitasking more efficient. Ergonomic office furniture also plays its part, fostering a comfortable and sustainable working environment that mitigates the physical stresses of sitting or standing for long periods.

Your smartphone or tablet becomes a versatile extension of your workspace. With apps for email, project management, and communication, you remain connected and responsive even when you're on the move. These devices embody the flexibility that remote work champions, allowing you to transition smoothly between tasks and environments.

Lastly, consider cybersecurity tools such as VPNs, firewalls, and antivirus software. Protecting sensitive data and maintaining privacy is essential, given the variety of networks we connect to throughout the day. These tools offer peace of mind and safeguard both personal and professional information.

In conclusion, a well-curated set of tools equips you to navigate the demands of remote work with confidence and efficiency. The right combination supports productivity, communication, and security, empowering you to focus on what truly matters—achieving your best work in a setting that's uniquely your own.

## Home Office Design for Maximum Productivity

In an era where the dining table often doubles as a desk and the coziness of home sometimes blurs the lines between relaxation and productivity, designing an effective home office becomes paramount. Crafting a workspace that stimulates creativity, enhances focus, and supports sustained productivity isn't just about aesthetics—it's about creating an environment where you can thrive.

First, consider the location of your home office. It might be tempting to set up shop in the living room or kitchen, but these high-traffic areas can introduce distractions. Aim for a quiet, well-lit area where you can control the noise level. If a separate room isn't available, use partitions or room dividers to carve out your work zone. The ability to mentally and physically separate work from home life is a key component in maximizing productivity and maintaining work-life balance.

The visual appeal of your workspace can also have a profound impact on your mindset. Choose colors and decor that inspire and motivate you. While bright shades such as yellow or orange can energize, softer tones like blue or green can calm and focus the mind. The goal is to create a space that resonates with you personally, reminding you of your professional goals and aspirations. A simple, clutter-free zone can reduce mental distractions and allow for deeper concentration on tasks.

Ergonomics plays a crucial role in home office design. Investing in a good-quality office chair and desk isn't a luxury—it's a necessity. Your furniture should support good posture and provide comfort during long hours of work. The desk height should allow your forearms to rest parallel to the floor, and your computer screen should be at eye level to prevent neck strain. Ergonomically designed equipment can prevent health issues and boost productivity significantly.

Lighting is another critical element often overlooked in home office design. Natural light is ideal, as it helps regulate mood and enhances alertness. Position your desk near a window if possible, but be mindful of glare on your computer screen. Supplement natural light with layered artificial lighting strategies: overhead lights for general illumination, desk lamps for task lighting, and ambient lighting to create a balanced visual environment. Avoid harsh lighting that can cause eye strain.

Let's not forget the importance of personalizing your workspace. Surrounding yourself with motivational quotes, artworks, or plants can create a sense of ownership and motivation. Plants, for instance, can boost air quality and bring a touch of nature into your space. Personal touches help to imbue a sense of identity to your workspace, which can, in turn, foster greater affiliation and motivation while working from home.

Space organization is also on the checklist for an efficient home office. Use shelves, cabinets, and organizers to keep your workspace tidy. Implementing a filing system will prevent paper clutter from overtaking your desk. Organize digital files as well to streamline workflow and easily access what you need without unnecessary time-wasting. An organized space often reflects an organized mind, increasing productivity and reducing stress.

Sound control can further enhance your focus. If absolute silence is your match made in heaven, noise-canceling headphones might be a worth-while investment. For those who thrive with a bit of background noise, gentle music or ambient sounds can mask interruptions. The key is to identify what auditory environment works best for you and adjust your home office design accordingly.

Creating a dynamic setup can keep you engaged and energized throughout the day. Consider a standing desk or adjustable workstation, allowing you to switch between sitting and standing. This flexibility can be a game-changer in maintaining both physical well-being and productivity throughout the workday. Additionally, the introduction of movement—even if it's just standing and stretching—can refresh your concentration and prevent fatigue.

Finally, technology should support, not hinder, your productivity. Ensure you have access to all the essential tools and a reliable internet connection to minimize technical disruptions. Cable management systems can prevent cords from tangling and keep your desk looking clean and professional. Smart home devices, ergonomic peripherals, and dual monitors can enhance your work efficiency and comfort.

In designing a home office for maximum productivity, it's not just about the physical space—it's about creating an environment that aligns with your rhythms and work style. It's about balance, personalization, and, ultimately, setting the stage where you can do your best work, every single day.

# Chapter 3: Technology and Connectivity

In the vibrant world of remote work, technology and connectivity are our trusty allies, empowering us to transcend boundaries and seamlessly weave our tasks into the fabric of our daily lives. It's more than just having the latest gadgets—it's about a harmonious blend of tools tailored to your needs, enabling a productive and fulfilling work experience from any corner of the globe. Your devices don't just facilitate work; they transform how you interact with your colleagues, deliver results, and shape your day-to-day experiences.

Choosing the right technology can feel overwhelming with so many options at your fingertips. Think of them not just as tools, but as extensions of your professional self. Would a high-powered laptop enhance your capability to perform complex tasks with ease? Or perhaps a tablet for on-the-go productivity suits your lifestyle better? Consider how each device aligns with your work requirements and personal workflow. Investing time into understanding your tech needs can lead to a smoother and more rewarding remote working journey.

Beyond devices, connectivity is the glue that holds the remote work structure together. A reliable internet connection is paramount. Imagine struggling with a connection that falters during crucial video calls or fails to upload important documents. Prioritizing stable internet service ensures you stay connected without interruption, enabling fluid communication and uninterrupted focus. It's about laying a digital foundation so robust that it leaves you free to concentrate on what truly matters—your work and professional growth.

Harnessing the power of technology and connectivity effectively is about transforming challenges into opportunities. With the right setup, you're not just meeting expectations but potentially exceeding them. Embrace these tools as collaborators in your remote work journey, and let them propel your career to new heights while maintaining a sense of personal balance and satisfaction. With the right mindset, technology becomes not just an enabler but a catalyst for success in your remote work endeavors.

## Choosing the Right Devices

As you dive deeper into the world of remote work, choosing the right devices becomes paramount to your success. The devices you select are more than just tools; they're the very foundation upon which you build your productivity and maintain your connectivity. In today's digital landscape, remote work demands a synergy between functionality and flexibility. With every keystroke and video call, the efficiency of your device can either propel you towards success or drag you into frustration. With the plethora of options available, how do you know which ones are right for you?

First, consider your specific needs as a remote worker. Different roles may require different technological capabilities. A graphic designer might need a high-resolution monitor and a computer with powerful graphics processing, while a writer could thrive with a lightweight laptop optimized for word processing and uninterrupted internet access. Reflect on the nature of your work—if it involves frequent virtual meetings, then a device with a clear and reliable webcam and microphone will serve you well. Identifying these needs will form the cornerstone of an informed decision.

Mobility is another critical factor. The beauty of remote work lies in its flexibility, allowing you to work from various locations. A portable device that doesn't compromise on power can be a game-changer. Laptops are often the go-to choice due to their balance between performance and portability. For a truly mobile lifestyle, consider devices with longer battery life to avoid the constant search for power outlets. Tablets, equipped with detachable keyboards, offer another layer of versatility, particularly when paired with cloud-based applications that sync seamlessly across multiple devices.

However, don't overlook the importance of ergonomics and comfort—long hours spent in front of a screen can take a toll on your health if your setup isn't conducive to your well-being. Choosing devices that allow you to maintain a posture-friendly environment is key. External keyboards and mice can be valuable additions, allowing you to arrange your workspace in an ergonomically efficient manner, reminiscent of traditional office settings.

When assessing options, the importance of software compatibility and ecosystem integration cannot be overstated. If you're invested in a particular operating system, select devices that integrate smoothly within that ecosystem to avoid compatibility issues. Your smartphone, tablet, and computer should ideally work in harmony, enabling seamless transitions between tasks and minimizing interruptions. This cohesion often simplifies troubleshooting and enhances user experience, allowing you to focus more on your work than on your tools.

Let's not forget about storage solutions—cloud storage has revolutionized the way we store and access files, offering a viable alternative to traditional hard drive storage. With cloud solutions, your documents are accessible anywhere, anytime, which is perfect for the remote worker prone to switch locations. Opt for devices that easily sync with your chosen cloud service, ensuring that your workflow isn't disrupted by storage limitations.

Security should also be a top priority. Protecting sensitive work data is non-negotiable. Devices with built-in security features, such as biometric authentication and encrypted storage, add an extra layer of protection against cyber threats. This is particularly relevant if you handle confidential materials or work for organizations with strict data governance policies. Investing in a secure device is an investment in peace of mind.

Budget constraints may influence your decision-making process, but it's crucial to view technology not just as an expense, but as an investment. The right device will not only last longer but can significantly boost your productivity and quality of work. Don't compromise on core features that are essential to your role, and prioritize functionality over superficial extras. Often, mid-range devices offer an impressive feature set that caters well to remote work requirements without breaking the bank.

Incorporating device assessments into your decision-making may also include looking at reviews and seeking recommendations from fellow remote workers. They can provide insights and real-world perspectives on what has worked well in diverse remote work settings. Community and peer feedback can be invaluable in guiding your choices, offering a pragmatic view that specifications alone may not fully capture.

Once you've chosen your devices, remember that your relationship with technology is a dynamic one. Regular updates and routine maintenance are essential to ensuring your devices remain reliable over time. Automation tools and software updates can enhance performance and resolve potential compatibility issues, paving the path for future scalability and adaptiveness. Embrace these updates as part of your strategy to remain cutting-edge in an ever-evolving digital workplace.

Ultimately, the right device is a powerful ally in your remote work journey, one that ensures you're not just keeping up with the demands of your work but excelling in it. The effort invested in choosing the right tools now will pay dividends as you navigate the diverse challenges and opportunities that remote work brings.

# Ensuring a Reliable Internet Connection

In the realm of remote work, a reliable internet connection isn't just a convenience—it's the backbone of your professional existence. Imagine gearing up for an important presentation, only to face intermittent connectivity issues that cause video calls to lag and files to upload at a snail's pace. The frustration is palpable, and it's a disruption no remote worker can afford. Therefore, securing a dependable internet connection is critical to maintaining productivity and staying connected with colleagues across the globe.

The internet is our gateway to work, collaboration, and even management software. It stands to reason, then, that understanding and optimizing your home network should be a priority. Start by assessing your needs. Are you someone who regularly hosts webinars or video conferences? Or perhaps you rely on large data transfers? Your internet package should align with these requirements. Bandwidth and speed are pivotal; ensure your plan can comfortably support your work activities without frequent buffering or dropouts.

Beyond the choice of service, consider the physical hardware that makes up your local network. Routers are often overlooked but play a significant role in internet performance. Investing in a high-quality router can dramatically enhance your internet's speed and reliability. Pay attention to the placement of this hardware. Positioning your router in a central location minimizes dead zones, ensuring stable connectivity throughout your home office. This small tweak can make a big difference, especially in homes with multiple users or numerous devices.

For those working in areas where wired connections are feasible, an Ethernet cable can provide the most stable and fastest connection possible. Unlike Wi-Fi, which can be subject to interference from walls and other devices, a wired connection can enhance both reliability and speed. It's a straightforward way to minimize fluctuations, especially during tasks that demand high bandwidth.

Then, there's the practical consideration of backup solutions. No matter how reliable your primary connection is, outages can happen, often at the most inconvenient times. Consider secondary options like mobile hotspots, which can be a lifesaver when your regular service goes down. Many smartphones have this functionality built-in, and it's worthwhile to familiarize yourself with these features ahead of time.

Cloud-based tools and collaborative platforms necessitate a stable connection. Lag or downtime here could mean missed messages, synchronization failures, or even data loss—all scenarios best avoided. Regularly testing your internet speed and connection strength can help identify problems before they dramatically impact your workflow. Utilize tools like speed tests and network diagnostic software to stay informed about your connection's performance.

But what if optimizing your internet seems out of reach due to location-based limitations? Satellite internet or other remote-area solutions may offer viable alternatives to traditional broadband services. While often accompanied by higher latency, these options are steadily improving in terms of speed and reliability. They can serve as crucial fallback measures for those living in areas underserved by cable and fiber networks.

Another strategy to consider is leveraging virtual private network (VPN) services. Not only do these enhance security by encrypting data, but they also often provide more consistent connectivity by connecting to less-congested routing paths. This can be particularly useful if you're in a residential area prone to bandwidth throttling during peak times.

The emotional aspect of connectivity in remote work shouldn't be ignored either. Unstable internet can be a cause of significant stress and distraction. Knowing that meetings can proceed smoothly contributes to a sense of professional competence and peace of mind. This reliability allows you to focus on your tasks without the underlying worry of tech-induced interruptions.

Balancing redundancy and reliability with cost-effectiveness is an ongoing challenge, but one worth addressing. If feasible, negotiate with your internet service provider for better packages or service guarantees. They may offer incentives for long-term commitments or provide discounts if you're bundling with other services.

Keep abreast of technological advancements in the connectivity field. New technologies frequently emerge, offering promise in reliability and speed, often at reduced costs. Tech reviews and consumer advice columns can be rich resources for identifying future-proof hardware and services that match a remote worker's unique demands.

Establishing a reliable internet connection for remote work is as much about foresight as it is about current needs. Integrating forward-thinking solutions ensures you're not only meeting today's demands but are also prepared for tomorrow's challenges. As an integral pillar of remote work, reliable connectivity empowers you to expand your horizons, connect seamlessly, and focus on what truly matters: delivering your best work, no matter where you are.

# Chapter 4: Time Management Strategies

Time management doesn't just happen; it's crafted carefully, especially in a remote work environment where boundaries blur. It might often feel like the day races ahead of you, but remember, you've got the power to steer it. Successful remote workers deploy strategies that are more art than science, enabling them to harness their most precious resource: time.

One of the foundational steps is setting clear priorities. Start with the tasks that align most closely with your objectives and deadlines, letting go of the less crucial or delegating when possible. Installing a system like the Eisenhower Box or even a simple to-do list can make all the difference. By visualizing tasks, you can better grasp what needs immediate attention and what can wait, ultimately driving your productivity up while stress levels dive down.

Another strategy involves tackling procrastination, which can silently erode your workday. Understanding the root of your procrastination is the key—often it's not laziness but rather fear of imperfection or feeling overwhelmed. Breaking tasks into manageable chunks can counteract this. Implementing techniques such as the Pomodoro Technique—focused work periods followed by short breaks—enables a steady rhythm of productivity, making daunting tasks more palatable and less intimidating.

No strategy is complete without considering the environment. The physical setup influences mental clarity. Designate specific blocks of time for focused work, and ensure your workspace signals your brain that it's time to focus. Couple this with regular check-ins using a calendar tool to keep track and recalibrate as necessary. These adaptations promote not just efficient management of tasks but also carve out necessary personal time, ensuring a balanced approach to the workday.

The path to mastering time management in remote work isn't linear. It requires patience, discipline, and adaptability. By employing these strategies, you not only enhance your productivity but also foster a healthier work-life synergy, fostering an environment where success and well-being walk hand-in-hand.

## Prioritizing Tasks Effectively

In the dynamic world of remote work, where distractions lurk around every corner and emails ping incessantly, mastering the art of prioritizing tasks isn't just a skill—it's a necessity. Effective task prioritization acts as your guiding compass, steering you effortlessly through the myriad of responsibilities competing for your attention. But how exactly do you decide what deserves your attention first? And how do you balance this with the unpredictability of a decentralized work environment? Let's delve into this.

The key to prioritizing effectively starts with crystal clarity on your objectives. Success comes from moving the needle on tasks that truly matter, not just those that scream for attention. This requires a clear understanding of your goals and aligning your daily activities with them. Reflect on your current initiatives and long-term goals. Ensure that every task maps directly to these objectives, acting as stepping stones towards achieving them.

Next, embrace the Eisenhower Box, an age-old but still invaluable principle. This technique classifies tasks based on urgency and importance, helping you distinguish between what needs immediate attention, what can be scheduled for later, delegated, or even eliminated entirely. Imagine your to-do list divided into four quadrants—those that are urgent and important, important but not urgent, urgent but not important, and neither urgent nor important. Channel your energy into tasks that are both urgent and important; these drive immediate and meaningful progress.

However, distinguishing between urgencies and importance can sometimes be tricky, especially when working remotely. The flexibility of remote work often blurs lines, causing everything to feel urgent. Herein lies the magic of intentionality. Always ask yourself: "Is this task moving me closer to my key objectives?" If the answer is no, reconsider its place on your list. The power of "no" should be wielded wisely but effectively.

Remote workers often find themselves juggling multiple projects across varied timelines. Here, task batching emerges as a superpower. Batching involves grouping similar tasks and tackling them in focused, uninterrupted sessions. This minimizes the cognitive load associated with switching between disparate activities. Regularly check off similar tasks like emails, reports, or team updates. Not only does this enhance focus, but it also boosts your efficiency by eliminating constant context switching.

Within a remote team setting, clear communication becomes a pivotal tool for task prioritization. Regular check-ins and updates can help synchronize priorities across different time zones and individual schedules. Managers should earnestly encourage team members to voice roadblocks and resource requirements. When everyone knows what others are working on, it facilitates a more cohesive approach to prioritization, ensuring that crucial tasks aren't overlooked.

Despite your best efforts to prioritize, unexpected challenges are inevitable. Flexibility remains integral to any effective prioritization strategy. Be prepared to re-evaluate and reorganize based on the dynamic nature of projects and remote collaborations. Real-time adjustments should be embraced, not feared. To manage this, combine agile methodologies with your prioritization routine, allowing for iterative re-assessment of ongoing tasks and priorities.

Technology provides an arsenal of tools to enhance your prioritization efforts. Project management platforms, like Trello or Asana, offer intuitive ways to organize and track tasks. These tools provide a visual map of your responsibilities, enabling quick assessments and adjustments. Set reminders and deadlines within these platforms, ensuring that nothing slips through the cracks.

An underrated element of effective prioritization is self-awareness. Understanding when you're most productive can radically improve how you tackle tasks. Some people thrive in the morning light, while others hit their stride after lunch or even late at night. Once you determine your peak performance hours, prioritize high-impact tasks during this time. Reserve administrative or less creative tasks for when your energy might naturally wane.

Regularly review and reflect on your prioritization strategies. What's working? What's not? In a remote environment, it's easy to get lost in day-to-day execution without halting to reassess the path. Schedule frequent reviews to evaluate your strategies, ensuring they align with your desired outcomes. This helps catch inefficiencies early and reinforces positive habits over time.

Lastly, don't underestimate the power of recharging. Breaks aren't an indulgence, they're a necessity. Stepping away helps sustain focus and productivity over longer periods. Implement techniques like the Pomodoro Technique, which alternates intense focus sessions with short breaks. This helps manage mental fatigue, allowing you to return to your task list with renewed vigor and clarity.

In conclusion, remote work equips you with the freedom to design your workday, but with that freedom comes the responsibility of intentional task management. By identifying what truly matters, leveraging the right tools, and nurturing clear communication, you'll be able to cut through the noise and lead your remote work experience with purpose. Task prioritization might be an art, but it's one that brings immense rewards when mastered.

## Overcoming Procrastination

We've all faced that moment when a task sits on your to-do list for what seems like an eternity. Instead of tackling it right away, you shuffle it to the bottom, hoping somehow it'll just disappear. In remote work, procrastination has a sneaky way of disguising itself. Without the physical presence of colleagues or the tangible office environment, the cues to get started can easily blur. But overcoming procrastination isn't just about getting things done. It's about reclaiming control over your time and energy, allowing space for creativity, and ultimately thriving in your remote work setting.

At the heart of procrastination lies a complex interplay of emotions. Often, it's not laziness that leads us to my procrastinate, but rather fear of failure or a lack of clarity about the next steps. Recognizing these emotions is the first move toward change. Cultivating self-awareness helps you identify triggers, making it easier to address them head-on. Equipping yourself with strategies to overcome procrastination involves both emotional intelligence and practical techniques.

A tried-and-true strategy for battling procrastination is breaking tasks into smaller, more manageable chunks. This process, known as "chunking", transforms a daunting project into a series of approachable actions. For example, instead of viewing an entire project as one task, redefine it into sections like research, outlining, writing, and editing. Each small victory propels you forward, fostering momentum and diminishing the mountain of work into a series of achievable steps.

Another effective approach is the Pomodoro Technique, a time management method that encourages working in focused bursts with scheduled breaks. This technique leverages the power of time constraints to boost productivity. By working intently for 25 minutes and then taking a five-minute break, you train your brain to maintain high levels of concentration while also allowing time for mental rejuvenation. These intervals not only prevent burnout but also make starting a task feel less overwhelming.

Creating accountability can be a game-changer in a remote setting. Share your goals and timelines with a colleague or friend. This external accountability adds an extra layer of motivation. Knowing someone else is aware of your deadlines can drive you to stay on track. Additionally, consider digital accountability tools that remind you of your commitments, track your progress, and celebrate accomplishments along the way.

Embrace the power of setting clear, specific goals at the start of your day or week. The more defined your objectives, the easier it is to focus your efforts effectively. Consider adopting the SMART criteria—Specific, Measurable, Achievable, Relevant, and Time-bound. When goals are aligned with these parameters, they're more likely to be attainable and motivating.

Environment plays a pivotal role in combating procrastination. Remote workers have the unique advantage of customizing their workspaces. Establish a designated work area that signals productivity when you sit down to work. Remove distractions, and ensure the tools and resources you need are easily accessible. Creating an environment conducive to work can mentally prepare you to jump into tasks more readily.

The role of self-compassion cannot be understated in this battle. There will be days when procrastination wins; this is a natural part of the human experience. Be kind to yourself and avoid harsh self-criticism. Accept these moments as opportunities to learn and adjust your strategies. Reflect on what led to the procrastination and how you can better align your intentions with your actions in the future.

Meditation and mindfulness practices are also effective tools for maintaining focus and reducing procrastination. These practices increase your awareness of the present moment, enabling you to notice when your mind wanders. By anchoring your attention to the task at hand, you can halt the drift into procrastination and guide yourself back to productivity.

Consider the power of deadlines. Not all tasks in remote work come with a clear-cut due date, which can sometimes lead to indefinite postponement. When deadlines are absent, create your own. Self-imposed deadlines, accompanied by a completion schedule, can provide the structure and urgency needed to complete tasks on time. Pairing deadlines with rewards can further heighten motivation.

Above all, celebrate your achievements, no matter how small. Recognition and celebration of completed tasks can solidify positive reinforcement. This habit not only boosts morale but can also strengthen your resolve against procrastination. Whether it's a small break, a walk, or an indulgent treat, rewards provide a satisfying conclusion to your efforts.

In tackling procrastination, remote workers showcase resilience and adaptability. With the right mindset and tools, it's possible to transform the inefficiencies of procrastination into opportunities for growth. Mastering this art enables you to seize control over your workday, paving the way for enhanced productivity and the fulfillment that accompanies completing a day's work purposefully.

Tackling procrastination doesn't require perfection—just consistent effort. Embrace this journey, and with each step, you get closer not just to checked boxes but to a more intentional, rewarding remote work life.

# Chapter 5: Maintaining Work-Life Balance

As remote work becomes the norm for many, the line between personal life and work often blurs. It's vital to carve out a space where one begins and the other ends. Remote workers, whether freelancers or team managers, thrive on the freedom and flexibility this lifestyle provides, yet the challenge lies in maintaining a healthy work-life balance. That is why setting clear boundaries is essential. Knowing when to turn off work-related notifications and when to step away from your home office can make all the difference.

Creating a daily routine that includes both work and personal time is crucial. It doesn't need to be rigid, but having a rhythm helps in preventing work hours from bleeding into personal time. For instance, start the day with activities that refresh the mind, like exercise or meditation. Setting aside moments solely dedicated to family, friends, and hobbies is equally important, nurturing relationships that are just as significant as professional responsibilities. These moments of connection can rejuvenate and prepare you to tackle your tasks with renewed vigor.

One effective strategy is to designate a specific workspace within your home. This not only aids focus but also helps in mentally disconnecting from work when you leave that area. It could be a spare room or simply a corner in your living room; what's important is that when you step away, you're leaving work behind. If possible, have separate devices for work and personal use, so you're not tempted to check emails during downtime.

Lastly, remember that balance is more about fluidity than strict separation. Embrace the ability to adjust your schedule according to your needs, whether that means starting earlier some days to catch an evening event or taking a mid-day break. When remote work aligns with your lifestyle, it fuels personal satisfaction and leads to sustainable productivity in the long run.

## Creating Boundaries Between Work and Home

In today's increasingly digital world, where work often blurs into personal life, establishing firm boundaries between work and home is crucial. Without these boundaries, remote workers may find their days stretching endlessly, leading to burnout and reduced productivity. The challenge isn't just about partitioning physical space; it requires a disciplined mindset to separate professional responsibilities from personal time. Achieving this separation is more of a necessity than a luxury, pivotal for nurturing mental health and ensuring work satisfaction.

One of the foundational steps to draw clear lines between work and home life is adopting a structured routine. For many remote workers, the absence of a commute might seem like a gift, providing extra time. However, this can quickly turn into a double-edged sword. Routines help signal to your brain when it's time to shift gears between work mode and home mode. Consider setting fixed start and end times for your workday. Physically changing your environment at the beginning and end of the day, like taking a short walk, can also reinforce this transition.

Additionally, designing a designated workspace is critical. Ideally, this should be a space with minimal distractions and one you can leave at the end of your workday. For those with limited space, even a small desk in a corner or a specific chair can be enough to create this boundary. The key is to psychologically link this space with working, making it distinct from other areas of your home.

Managing notifications and digital interruptions plays a significant role in maintaining boundaries. With emails, messages, and virtual meetings, it's all too easy to slip back into work mode even when you're off the clock. Establishing clear rules about when you check emails or messages can help. Tools like apps or software that block certain notifications during non-working hours can provide a buffer, letting you focus on personal time without digital distractions.

Create rituals that signify the end of your work day. Whether it's shutting down your computer, changing your clothes, or engaging in a brief meditation session, these rituals can help signal to your mind and body that it's time to step away from work tasks. Such practices can make it easier to unwind and mentally detach from work-related stressors.

Communication is also important in maintaining these boundaries. Inform your colleagues and clients about your working hours and your preference for communication within these times. When expectations are clearly set and adhered to, it reduces the pressure to be perpetually available, allowing you to disconnect without guilt.

It's crucial to regularly assess your boundaries for effectiveness. Just as a leak can gradually diminish the integrity of a dam, ineffective boundaries might slowly let work seep into personal time. Schedule reflections, perhaps weekly or monthly, to evaluate how your boundaries are holding up. Adjust and adapt as necessary, especially as your work responsibilities and personal life evolve.

Another strategy involves consciously scheduling time to connect with others. Social interaction is often missing in remote work, leading to feelings of isolation that can prompt overworking as a distraction. Building regular check-ins with friends or family into your schedule strengthens the home aspect of work-life balance. It reminds you that time spent away from the desk is not just permissible—it's essential.

Self-care activities should also be deliberately incorporated into your routine. Whether it's exercise, reading, or pursuing a hobby, these activities replenish your energy and creativity, ensuring you approach your work refreshed and motivated. By prioritizing personal time, you reinforce the importance of maintaining a clear demarcation between work and home.

There's also a need to reevaluate technology use outside work hours. Limiting screen time can contribute significantly to a healthier home environment. Engage in activities that don't involve screens to provide a genuine break from the digital interface that dominates your workday. Reading a book, cooking, or even tackling a home improvement project can be fulfilling ways to shift focus and relax.

The concept of boundaries can extend to thought patterns, too. Remote workers may find their minds drifting back to work tasks or concerns even during personal time, especially if transitions have been inconsistent. Practicing mindfulness or meditation can be effective in observing these thoughts without judgment and gently steering your mind back to the present moment.

Lastly, keep in mind that boundaries are not a one-time set-and-forget solution. They are dynamic and might require ongoing fine-tuning. Be flexible and patient with yourself as you find what works best. Every individual and family might require different techniques to maintain harmony between work and home life.

To conclude, creating boundaries between work and home is not simply about drawing lines; it's about crafting a lifestyle that supports your well-being, productivity, and happiness. These boundaries act as safeguards, allowing you to thrive both personally and professionally, ensuring that neither sphere overshadows the other. Embrace the process, and remember, the goal is a balanced integration of work into life—not the other way around.

## Strategies for Disconnecting

As remote work blurs the boundaries between professional obligations and personal life, disconnecting from work requires deliberate effort. It's more than simply shutting down your laptop at the end of the day; true disconnection involves mentally shifting away from work mode. This shift is crucial for maintaining your overall well-being and recharging for the days ahead. Let's explore strategies that can help you create those much-needed boundaries, ensuring a healthier balance between work and life.

One of the most effective strategies for disconnecting is setting clear work hours. While flexibility is a hallmark of remote work, it's essential to establish boundaries around your workday. Communicate your working hours to colleagues and clients, ensuring they respect your time outside these boundaries. This clear delineation allows you to focus on personal pursuits when the workday ends. A well-defined schedule not only facilitates disconnection but also enhances productivity during work hours.

Consider implementing a daily shutdown routine. This routine can signal the end of your workday, helping your brain to transition from work mode to personal time. It might include activities like reviewing your task list, organizing your workspace, and powering down your devices. Over time, this practice becomes a powerful mental cue that tells your brain it's time to relax and focus on non-work-related pursuits. Such rituals create a boundary that separates your professional and personal life.

While technology connects us in incredible ways, it can also tether us to work outside normal hours. To truly disconnect, it may be necessary to establish tech-free zones and times during your day. Designate areas in your home where work gadgets are off-limits. Similarly, choose specific times where you check and respond to work-related communications. By creating these tech-free buffers, you give yourself permission to engage fully in your personal life without distractions or interruptions.

Detaching from work is also about engaging with activities that enrich and fulfill you. Hobbies, social interactions, and physical activities can be excellent ways to shift your focus away from work. Join a local club, take up gardening, or perhaps indulge in cooking. These activities allow your mind to engage in different patterns of thinking, offering a refreshing break from your usual work routine. Connections formed through these activities often lead to enhanced life satisfaction and improved mental health.

Mindfulness and meditation offer beneficial ways to disconnect from the stresses of work. Spending even a few minutes a day in meditation can help clear your mind and bring a sense of peace, making it easier to detach from work obligations. Mindful practices increase your awareness of the present moment, preventing work thoughts from encroaching on your personal time. This approach gradually trains your mind to let go of work during non-work hours effectively.

Think about taking time to unplug completely. Sabbaticals or extended digital detoxes might be challenging to integrate into a busy schedule, but they can provide profound benefits. A weekend camping trip or a week-long vacation without checking emails may sound radical, but such breaks can dramatically enhance your creativity and productivity once you return. You'll find that these types of breaks are both a reward for hard work and a necessary part of maintaining long-term motivation.

Another aspect to consider is compartmentalizing your digital life. Create separate email accounts for work and personal use, and be disciplined about which one you're accessing at the moment. By focusing on different email accounts based on the time of the day, you allow yourself to engage with tasks connected to either work or leisure without blending them. This separation helps reinforce boundaries and contributes significantly to maintaining work-life balance.

Let's not forget the power of physical environments on our mental state. Creating dedicated spaces for work and relaxation can reinforce your mental boundaries. If possible, try to keep your work area separate from spaces meant for relaxation and leisure. Transitioning from your home office to your living room, for example, can symbolize leaving work behind and entering a space designated for unwinding.

Lastly, make use of support networks. Talking to friends, family, or other remote workers about the challenge of disconnecting can lead to shared solutions and insights. Support groups offer both accountability and encouragement, reminding you that others, too, face similar challenges. Connecting with those who understand your situation often leads to innovative strategies for disconnecting effectively, making this a vital component of maintaining work-life balance.

By implementing these strategies, remote workers, freelancers, and managers can ensure they disconnect effectively from work-related demands. In doing so, they safeguard their well-being, ultimately leading to more fulfilling personal lives and more productive work experiences. Remember, disconnecting from work isn't about neglecting responsibilities; it's about recharging to tackle them with renewed energy and focus.

# Chapter 6: Communication in a Remote World

In today's remote work landscape, communication has become the bedrock of success. When physical office walls vanish, the challenge is to maintain clarity, understanding, and connection across digital divides. It's essential to not only understand how to use these tools but also to leverage them effectively. Consider the myriad of platforms at your disposal—emails to instant messages, video calls to collaborative boards. Each one offers unique strengths for a specific kind of communication. Identifying the right tool for the right message can make all the difference in maintaining smooth operations and fostering team cohesion.

To thrive in this environment, cultivating strong communication skills tailored to a virtual realm is paramount. It's not just about typing faster or learning how to use a new app; it's about truly connecting with your audience. Pay attention to tone, clarity, and context to ensure that your message is received as intended. Active listening, even over a headset, is critical. Ensure that you're engaging with others' inputs and making them feel heard, respected, and valued. Remember, communication is a two-way street, and feedback is as vital as information sharing.

Empathy plays a significant role too. In a decentralized setup, empathy bridges the gap between colleagues spread across different time zones and cultures. By understanding and respecting various perspectives, you enrich workplace dialogues and deepen interpersonal connections. Communication isn't just about exchanging words; it's about building relationships and trust. This foundation is invaluable, especially when challenges arise.

Embrace the power of storytelling to engage and inspire. Stories forge connections, making data and updates more relatable and memorable. Whether you're leading a team meeting or catching up with a colleague, weaving narratives into your communication can drive engagement and motivate your colleagues to align with the shared vision of your workplace. By focusing on human elements within remote interactions, you build a resilient and dynamic work culture.

## Leveraging Digital Communication Tools

In the landscape of remote work, digital communication tools have become more than just a convenience—they are the lifeblood of effective collaboration and productivity. As we navigate the nuances of working from scattered geographies and time zones, leveraging these tools effectively can spell the difference between floundering and thriving. The purpose of this exploration is to not only familiarize you with these tools but to also shed light on strategies that maximize their advantages and minimize potential pitfalls.

To start with, the breadth and variety of digital communication channels are astonishing. From video calls to instant messaging, the choices feel endless. Finding the right set of tools for your team can feel daunting at first, but it's easier when you consider the unique needs of your team or project. Each tool offers distinct advantages: video conferencing emphasizes face-to-face interaction, while chat applications allow for quick, informal exchanges. Balancing these tools ensures the right message gets across in the right way.

**Video conferencing software** like Zoom, Microsoft Teams, or Google Meet has rapidly become a staple in remote work. These platforms break down geographical barriers, bridging teams with real-time visual interaction. They bring the essential human element back to remote work, helping to convey tone and emotion, components often lost in text communication. However, it's not just about hopping on calls. Successful teams plan structured meetings with clear agendas. This prevents the common problem of "meeting fatigue," ensuring discussions are purposeful and time-efficient.

Asynchronous communication also plays a pivotal role in remote work dynamics. Tools like Slack, Microsoft Teams chat, or similar platforms allow team members to interact without the pressure of immediate response. It respects individual work rhythms and time zones, fostering a more thoughtful and inclusive communication culture. Understanding when to shift from synchronous to asynchronous communication not only enhances productivity but also preserves the precious resource of time.

Beyond mainstream channels, project management tools integrate communication features that are indispensable for tracking progress and facilitating discussions tied directly to project needs. Applications like Asana, Trello, and Jira not only help in assigning tasks but also in ensuring that all discussions are context-bound and easily revisitable. When everyone has clear visibility of the project timeline and requirements, the likelihood of miscommunication is drastically reduced.

Yet, as we delve deeper into digital communication, it's crucial to address the *'human factor'*. Empathy and understanding can sometimes get lost behind a screen. Building a sense of connection and rapport should be a priority. Encourage small talk and personal exchanges, which can replicate in-office watercooler moments and strengthen team bonds.

Virtual team-building exercises, casual chat spaces, and scheduled informal sessions are just a few ways to nurture genuine relationships.

Security is another cornerstone principle when leveraging digital tools. As information is exchanged across platforms, often containing sensitive data, ensuring secure communication channels is vital. Utilize end-to-end encrypted tools where applicable, and build a culture of mindful security practices among team members. By understanding the potential risks and adopting preventive measures, you maintain trust and safeguard company integrity.

Furthermore, for managers and team leaders, investing time in becoming adept at these tools is essential. Leading by example not only boosts the technical fluency of the team but also demonstrates a commitment to efficient and meaningful communication. Training sessions, shared resources, and continuous learning opportunities can empower everyone to utilize these tools effectively and creatively.

We must also acknowledge the evolving nature of these platforms. Staying informed about new features and updates can significantly enhance your communication strategy. Most tools regularly release updates aimed at improving user experience, adding functionalities like auto-translations, meeting transcriptions, or even AI-driven insights. Keeping abreast of these can provide your team with an edge in efficient communication.

For freelancers and individuals, integrating these tools into daily operations can streamline client interactions and personal workflow management. Freelancers can use digital communication for polished presentations, quick updates, and effective collaboration on creative projects, thus broadening their client base and enhancing service delivery.

Lastly, as much as digital communication tools are a boon, they can also lead to constant connectivity pressures. Encourage a culture where 'offline' is respected as much as 'online.' Set boundaries around communication, such as response times and work-off hours, to support mental well-being and prevent burnout. Empower employees and yourself to disconnect, thus maintaining a healthy work-life balance.

Digital communication tools are the thread weaving remote teams together, and leveraging them is not merely about using them—it's about using them well. By choosing the right tools, cultivating empathetic communication, prioritizing security, and keeping an eye on innovation, you can create a dynamic communication environment that enhances productivity and fosters meaningful connections.

## Developing Effective Communication Skills

In today's remote work landscape, communication isn't just a skill—it's an art. Our digital era demands that we redefine how we convey ideas, express emotions, and foster connections. While technology bridges vast distances, the nuances of effective communication remain ever critical. It's not merely about exchanging information; it's about ensuring that messages are understood, inspiring collaboration and cooperation. With the right approach, remote communication can be as impactful and nuanced as face-to-face conversations.

To thrive, remote workers, freelancers, and managers must cultivate an array of communication techniques tailored to various platforms and situations. This begins by understanding the core principles of clarity and consistency. Because remote teams miss out on the tangible cues of body language, words must do more than carry weight—they must convey precision and intent. A well-structured email or message can mitigate misunderstandings and enhance mutual understanding, fostering a cohesive team dynamic.

Emotional intelligence is another cornerstone in effective communication. This isn't about diluting professionalism with sentimentality; rather, it's acknowledging the human element behind every screen. Remote workers often face isolation, and empathetic communication can bridge that gap. Listening actively and responding thoughtfully reinforces a sense of belonging and appreciation, crucial elements for enhancing morale and productivity.

One can't ignore the role of feedback in fostering effective communication. Constructive feedback, delivered with respect and specificity, empowers individuals to grow and improve. It creates an environment where ideas are freely shared, and challenges are openly discussed. Constructive criticism should open doors to dialogue and solutions, rather than closing them. In remote settings, periodic check-ins and virtual meetings dedicated to open conversations about challenges can maintain transparency and trust.

Leveraging different communication tools effectively also plays a significant role. Text-based communication like emails and instant messages require brevity and clarity. However, the absence of vocal tone and body language demands careful attention to language choice. When quick decision-making or brainstorming is needed, video communication platforms can bridge the gap, bringing faces and voices into collaboration, igniting creativity, and building camaraderie among team members.

Moreover, setting communication guidelines or protocols within remote teams can alleviate common pitfalls. Establishing expectations regarding response times, preferred mediums for certain tasks, and appropriate times for synchronous communication can help reduce unnecessary stress and confusion. These guidelines empower team members to manage their schedules effectively, ensuring work-life balance while maintaining a strong line of communication.

Written communication shines when detailed records are required. Documenting conversations and decisions not only serves as a point of reference for later but also ensures everyone remains on the same page, reducing the chance of miscommunications. Yet, this doesn't mean sacrificing personality in messaging. Even in written form, a human touch—whether it's a friendly greeting or a thoughtful sign-off—can make digital interactions more personable and less transactional.

Asynchronous communication gives team members the opportunity to digest information and respond thoughtfully, free from the pressure of immediate response. This is particularly beneficial for teams scattered across various time zones. However, an asynchronous approach demands clarity and complete context as the recipient lacks the opportunity to seek immediate clarification.

For leaders managing remote teams, communication isn't about directing but about leading through influencing. It's about showing vulnerability, demonstrating trust, and fostering a culture where team members feel valued and heard. Leaders should practice active listening, encourage open expression of ideas and concerns, and affirm contributions to fuel motivation and commitment.

Ultimately, developing effective communication skills is a journey, requiring continuous adaptation and learning. Regularly seeking feedback from peers can illuminate areas for personal growth and refinement. Engaging with training modules or workshops on communication excellence can provide valuable insights into best practices and emerging trends in remote work communication.

In a remote world, mastering the art of communication isn't just about ensuring workflow efficiency; it's about forging connections, building trust, and creating a supportive work environment that transcends physical boundaries. As remote work continues to evolve and become more ingrained in our professional lives, honing these skills will not only advance careers but also enrich professional and personal relationships. Embrace the challenge, for it holds the potential to transform not just how we work, but how we connect in a world increasingly without borders.

# Chapter 7: Collaborative Tools for Remote Teams

In the ever-expanding landscape of remote work, collaboration tools emerge as the digital threads weaving teams together. These tools don't just enable communication; they transform it, infusing daily interactions with a fluidity and dynamism that defy geographical boundaries. Successful remote teams leverage these platforms to create cohesive and productive work environments, catalyzing both individual and collective achievements. Selecting the right tools can feel overwhelming, but the key lies in aligning your team's needs with the functionality of the tools.

When scouting for the best collaboration platforms, consider factors such as usability, integration capabilities, and security. Platforms like Slack or Microsoft Teams facilitate instant communication while integrating seamlessly with other workplace apps. This integration ensures that team members can access everything they need without switching contexts. These tools evolve beyond mere communication—they become the backbone of collaborative workflows, fostering an environment where creativity and productivity thrive.

Optimizing team workflow with these tools involves more than just implementing them; it's about championing a culture of open communication and accountability. Use project management tools like Asana or Trello to keep tasks organized and deadlines visible. Encourage team members to engage regularly and share updates to ensure transparency and minimize misunderstandings. The ultimate goal of these tools is to empower teams to focus on what truly matters—delivering outstanding results while nurturing a collaborative spirit.

Empathy plays a crucial role here. A tool might be perfect for one team member but cumbersome for another. Thus, encouraging feedback and being adaptable will help you fine-tune the tools you use. Celebrate the diversity these platforms accommodate, allowing each person's uniqueness to enrich the team. This harmonious integration of tools and talent forms the bedrock upon which remote teams can build their success.

## Selecting the Best Collaboration Platforms

In the vast landscape of remote work, where connectivity and productivity are king, choosing the right collaboration platform often feels like picking a needle from a haystack. It's not just about finding something that works but finding a tool that enhances team synergy, boosts creativity and drives efficiency to new heights. But with countless options available in today's digital marketplace, how do you decide which platform is best for your team? The answer lies in evaluating your team's specific needs, understanding the tools' capabilities, and sometimes, embracing the idea that one size does not fit all.

The first step in selecting a collaboration platform is identifying your team's core collaboration needs. Is your primary goal to manage projects and tasks, or are you looking to streamline direct communication? Perhaps your focus is on document sharing and editing, or maybe you need a platform that integrates with the numerous applications your team already uses. Begin by creating a checklist of the absolute must-haves, as this will act as a guiding compass through your selection journey.

Once you've nailed down your needs, the next phase involves exploring the available options. Popular collaboration platforms like Slack, Microsoft Teams, and Trello each offer unique features designed to enhance different aspects of team collaboration. Platforms such as Asana excel in task management and workflow organization, while Zoom makes virtual meetings feel almost in-person. If real-time collaboration on documents is essential, Google Workspace's integration of apps like Google Docs and Sheets can be your go-to.

However, with the allure of multitude features also comes the pitfall of redundancy. It's essential to choose platforms that prevent rather than create friction within your workflows. The expression "Jack of all trades, master of none" aptly applies here. A platform adorned with a plethora of features isn't beneficial if these bloated features slow down your systems or, worse, drown users in complexity. That's why simplicity and ease of use are critical factors for ensuring that your chosen platform supports rather than hinders productivity.

Another crucial aspect to consider is compatibility with existing systems. A truly synergistic work environment arises when collaboration tools seamlessly integrate with the software and platforms your team is already using. For example, if your team relies heavily on the Microsoft suite, then MS Teams, with its native app integrations, can provide smooth connectivity and data flow. Compatibility should extend to mobile functionalities too, as the modern remote worker requires flexibility in accessing work from a multitude of devices.

Then there are security considerations to bear in mind, especially if your work involves confidential data. The last thing you need is for security breaches to compromise your tools and by extension, your peace of mind. Choose platforms that offer robust security protocols, including end-to-end encryption and multi-factor authentication. These features should not be secondary but a central part of your evaluation. Prioritize those platforms that keep sensitive information secured while allowing easy accessibility to authenticated users.

But don't stop at features and security; consider also the user interface and overall user experience. After all, employees are more likely to engage and find contentment in using tools that are well-designed and intuitive. Test platforms yourself or invite team members to try out free trials. Gather feedback to understand their likes and dislikes. Remember, the adoption of a new tool is successful only when the team fully embraces it without facing resistance or confusion.

Cost is yet another dimension to weigh in your decision, but be cautious not to make it the sole determinant. It's essential to balance cost against the platform's value and benefits. Low-cost solutions might offer initial savings but could result in additional hidden costs through productivity drops and time spent on workarounds or fixes. Higher-tier options might seem too extravagant but could offer efficiencies and capabilities that soon recoup these expenditures through boosting productivity and collaboration.

Once you've narrowed down your choices, dive deeper into each platform's customer support and available resources. A platform's utility diminishes if issues arise and you're left without timely assistance. Platforms with extensive help centers, user communities, and responsive customer service are invaluable for ensuring sustained, smooth usage. Resources such as webinars and tutorials can further maximize the platform's utilization, providing continuous education for your team.

Finally, flexibility and scalability are future-oriented factors that can't be overlooked. Remote teams are dynamic; they grow, shrink, change, and evolve. A platform that is flexible to accommodate shifts in team size and project demands becomes an asset. Scalable options allow your collaboration tools to grow alongside your team, preventing the need for disruptive changes down the line. Platforms offering modular pricing and customizable features can facilitate smooth transitions into whatever the future holds for your team.

Remember, choosing the best collaboration platform is not a one-time task but an ongoing process. As technology evolves and new tools emerge, stay open to exploring updates and innovations that might better serve your changing needs. Encourage your team to engage in regular evaluations of the current platform's effectiveness and remain vigilant to signs that switching tools could unlock greater productivity and satisfaction.

When you have a platform that fits your team's ethos and workflow as snugly as a puzzle piece, remote work transforms from a challenge into a boundless opportunity. The right tools effectively used empower each team member, drawing out the best in their talents and fostering a shared vision of what success can look like—one where distance is inconsequential, and collaboration becomes the thread that tightly weaves your team together.

## Optimizing Team Workflow

Optimizing team workflow in a remote setting isn't just about implementing tools. It's about fostering an environment where everyone can thrive, contribute efficiently, and feel connected despite physical distances. At the heart of every successful remote team lies a collaborative ecosystem designed to leverage individual strengths while aligning them towards common goals.

Remote work introduces unique challenges, such as different time zones, cultural differences, and diversely paced working styles. However, it also presents unparalleled opportunities for innovation and creativity. The key to unlocking this potential is establishing a fluid workflow that adapts to both the team's evolving needs and the technological landscape.

One of the critical components of a well-optimized workflow is establishing clear, shared goals. When each member knows what they're working towards, efforts become more directed, reducing unnecessary complexity. Regular check-ins and planning sessions can help maintain focus and provide opportunities for everyone to voice concerns or suggest improvements.

It's essential to incorporate flexibility into the workflow. Rigid structures work well in controlled environments but can stifle creativity and responsiveness in remote settings. Allowing team members some autonomy over how they achieve their tasks can lead to better job satisfaction and perhaps even a more efficient outcome. A balance between individual freedom and team alignment often yields the best results.

Technology plays a crucial role in optimizing remote team workflows. Document collaboration tools, project management software, and communication platforms need to be thoughtfully integrated into the team's operations. The aim is to make these tools work for you, simplifying complex processes, and eliminating bottlenecks. When tools are intuitive and easy to use, they enhance productivity rather than hinder it.

Diversifying communication methods is another critical aspect. While email and messaging apps are great for quick exchanges, video calls can provide a richer context and help types of communication that convey nuances better than text. Regularly scheduled video meetings can not only tackle immediate issues but also build a stronger sense of team camaraderie. It's all about finding the right balance between digital interactions that are productive and those that are overwhelming.

Transparency is vital in a remote work environment. An optimized workflow should include mechanisms for transparently sharing progress, successes, and setbacks. Using dashboards or project management tools that allow every team member to see updates and give feedback encourages accountability and helps everyone stay informed, reducing the chances of miscommunication.

Optimizing workflow isn't a one-time task—it's ongoing. Teams should be encouraged to regularly review their processes and adapt as necessary. Open dialogue about what's working and what's not can lead to significant improvements. Inviting suggestions from all team members, regardless of their role, can bring fresh ideas to the table and foster a culture of continuous improvement.

Emotionally intelligent leadership is another cornerstone of an optimized workflow. Leaders should be attuned to their team's dynamics and proactive in addressing any tensions or obstacles. Supporting team members, showing empathy, and valuing each person's contributions can go a long way in ensuring a productive and happy remote working environment.

Trust builds the foundation of any successful remote team workflow. When team members trust each other and their leaders, they are more willing to take risks, share ideas, and put forth their best effort. This trust translates into reduced supervision and healthier work relationships, allowing teams to operate smoothly even when apart.

Lastly, encourage continuous learning and development. Remote teams should be given opportunities to grow their skills, which not only boosts individual morale but also increases the collective expertise of the team. Whether through workshops, courses, or collaborative projects, fostering personal growth can directly contribute to more optimized work processes.

In conclusion, optimizing team workflow in a remote environment requires more than just implementing new software. It demands a holistic approach that combines clear communication, flexibility, emotional intelligence, and a culture of trust. With these elements in place, remote teams are not only capable of overcoming the challenges they face but can also unlock new levels of collaboration and innovation.

# Chapter 8: Building a Remote Work Community

In the vast and ever-changing landscape of remote work, cultivating a sense of community can transform an isolating experience into one brimming with connection and support. At its core, building a remote work community isn't just about professional networking—it's about creating a support network that fuels motivation and wellbeing. When individuals come together with shared interests and goals, productivity thrives, and the sense of belonging grows deeper.

Start by identifying spaces where you can connect with other remote workers. Online platforms like forums and groups on social media serve as fertile ground for remote networking. These virtual meeting spots often provide tips, resources, and discussions that enhance your remote work experience. Don't shy away from engaging in these communities—it can lead to collaborations or even lifelong friendships, enriching both your professional and personal life.

Consider participating in online communities tailored to your specific industry or interests. It's important to seek groups that resonate with your professional identity and values. These platforms enable you to ask questions, share your experiences, and learn from others who understand the unique challenges and opportunities of remote work. Remember, being active in these communities isn't just about what you can gain, but also about what you can contribute. Generosity and active participation can often bring unexpected rewards and recognition.

You might also explore virtual events like webinars, workshops, and networking meetups. These not only break the monotony of working in isolation but are an excellent way to forge connections over shared learning experiences. Events like these can introduce you to new ideas, ignite inspiration, and facilitate relationships that might not have sparked in traditional work settings.

Ultimately, a thriving remote work community arises from a blend of authenticity, engagement, and openness. It's a reciprocal journey—one that requires both giving and receiving. With the right mindset and approach, remote work can transform from a solitary task into a collective adventure full of shared growth and success.

## Networking with Other Remote Workers

In today's virtual world, networking with fellow remote workers can be both empowering and transformative. Building a strong network not only enhances your professional growth but also fosters a sense of community that's often missed in remote work settings. It's about connecting beyond the digital screen, creating lasting relationships that provide support, collaboration opportunities, and yes, even friendship.

Think about the power of a well-placed connection. Oftentimes in remote work, your network becomes your lifeline. Whether you're seeking advice on a challenging project or simply wanting a fresh perspective on an idea, having a network of like-minded professionals is invaluable. They can open doors to unexpected opportunities and help you build credibility in your field.

One of the first steps in networking as a remote worker is embracing digital forums and social media. Platforms like LinkedIn are essential; they offer a dynamic space for showcasing your skills, sharing achievements, and engaging with industry thought leaders. Joining professional groups or online forums dedicated to your field can provide targeted interactions that lead to valuable exchanges or partnerships. Participating in these discussions not only expands your network but helps you stay abreast of industry trends and challenges.

But don't just stop at digital platforms. Attend virtual conferences and webinars relevant to your industry. They're excellent for learning and engaging in real-time discussions with other attendees. Interactive sessions and Q&As at these events provide an avenue to make a quick yet lasting impression on potential collaborators. When possible, make a point to engage with speakers or peers whose insights resonate with you. Following up with a personalized message after the event is crucial to solidifying these connections.

For a more personal touch, consider arranging one-on-one virtual coffee chats. These informal meetings are a great way to get to know someone better without the pressure of a formal meeting. By approaching these interactions with a genuine interest in the other person's story and expertise, you lay the groundwork for a relationship built on mutual respect and understanding.

However, effective networking is not just about what you get. It's equally about what you give. Offering your knowledge, resources, or even just a listening ear can foster goodwill and establish you as a valuable contact. Over time, the value you provide will resonate with others, and you're likely to see those efforts reciprocated when you need them the most. Remember, networking is a two-way street.

An often-overlooked gem in remote networking is utilizing coworking spaces. Although remote work allows flexibility, coworking spaces offer a physical location to work alongside other remote professionals. These spaces typically host networking events and workshops, which provide an opportunity to meet individuals you might not encounter in your remote routine. Even an occasional visit can break the isolation of remote work and introduce you to potentially game-changing relationships.

The world of remote networking also includes participation in mastermind groups. These small, focused groups bring together professionals who meet regularly to share insights, provide support, and hold each other accountable. Being part of a mastermind group can not only push your boundaries and introduce you to new ideas, but also affirm your goals in a supportive environment. It's about creating a community that champions your success.

Furthermore, as you grow your network, make a conscious effort to cultivate diversity within it. Engaging with individuals from varied backgrounds, industries, and experience levels enriches your pool of knowledge and perspectives. This diversity can inspire innovation and provide unique solutions to problems that you might not encounter in a more homogenous group.

Perhaps one of the most rewarding aspects of networking as a remote worker is the potential for collaboration on projects that truly excite you. As these relationships evolve, they often lead to partnerships on initiatives that align with your passion and expertise. Working with others who share your enthusiasm can breathe new life into your approach and result in projects that are both fulfilling and impactful.

In summary, building a network as a remote worker goes beyond mere connection—it is an investment in your professional and personal journey. By actively engaging with peers, offering value, and seeking diverse interactions, you lay the foundation for a thriving remote work community. As the world of work continues to evolve, so too will the opportunities for rich, meaningful networking experiences. Embrace this interconnectedness—it just might lead you to unexpected heights in your remote career.

## Participating in Online Communities

Joining online communities can be a game-changer for remote workers, freelancers, and anyone navigating a decentralized work environment. These communities are buzzing hives of ideas, support, and opportunities, offering more than just a digital space to drop in and out of. They're places where authentic connections can be made, where resources are shared freely, and where collaboration can flourish beyond traditional office boundaries. These communities help bridge the gap that distance naturally creates when you're not sharing the same physical workspace.

Participating in an online community starts with identifying where your interests and professional pursuits align with existing groups. Platforms like LinkedIn, Slack, and Reddit offer myriad groups covering virtually every industry and niche you can think of. Some communities focus on specific technologies, while others cater to broader topics such as remote leadership, productivity hacks, or work-life balance. The key is to be purposeful in selecting a community that matches your career goals and personal interests.

Engaging meaningfully in online communities requires more than just lurking in the background. It involves active participation—asking questions, sharing knowledge, and contributing to discussions. The beauty of these spaces is that they often operate as knowledge exchanges, where the currency is helpful insights and authentic support. Those who give to the community usually receive in return, whether it's guidance on a complex problem or learning about job opportunities.

Creating an engaging and impactful profile is crucial when you're about to dive into an online community. Think of it as your digital handshake. A clear, professional profile picture coupled with a concise bio that articulates your expertise and interests sets the stage for meaningful interactions. Don't underestimate the power of introductions. A well-crafted "hello" post can open doors to new connections and collaborations.

One of the most rewarding aspects of participating in online communities is the opportunity for networking and building your professional circle. Unlike traditional networking events where time and geographical constraints can limit interactions, online platforms offer global access. You have the chance to connect with industry leaders, mentors, and peers from around the world. This can lead to collaborations, mentorship, and even friendships that enrich your professional and personal growth.

Moreover, online communities democratize access to resources and support. No matter where you are in the world, you can tap into a wealth of knowledge that might have been inaccessible otherwise. Whether it's a free webinar, a shared document on best practices, or live Q&A sessions with experts, the learning potential is enormous. Part of thriving in a remote world is leveraging these opportunities to continuously develop your skills and knowledge.

It's important to respect the norms and culture of each community you join. Every online group has its unique set of rules and expectations that members follow to ensure productive and respectful interactions. Take time to understand these guidelines and observe how seasoned members contribute to discussions. You're more likely to make a positive impact and build trust if you honor the community's ethos.

Online communities also provide an emotional anchor. Working remotely, especially in isolation, can sometimes feel like shouting into the void. Having a network of like-minded individuals who understand the challenges and triumphs of remote work can be incredibly reassuring. These spaces allow you to voice your struggles and celebrate your wins among those who genuinely understand your journey.

The spontaneity and serendipity of organic office conversations might be missing, but online communities offer a different kind of spontaneity—one of instant connections across time zones and cultures. You can jump into a conversation at any time, offering feedback or proposing new ideas, and receive thoughtful replies in return. The diversity of perspectives you encounter enriches your understanding and broadens your worldview.

As you become more comfortable within your chosen communities, consider taking on a more active role. Organizing virtual meetups, webinars, or panel discussions can enhance your visibility and establish you as a thought leader. Running a successful event or contributing to the community in a way that others find valuable can greatly boost your reputation and influence.

Bare in mind that while engaging in online communities is highly beneficial, it's important to strike a balance. It can be tempting to dive headlong into endless discussions and networks, but time is a finite resource. Be methodical about your contributions and interactions, ensuring they align with your objectives and don't detract from your primary work responsibilities. This balance is crucial for maintaining productivity.

Lastly, don't be afraid to create your own community if you see a gap in the existing landscape. Building a community from scratch allows you to shape the culture and focus on topics and issues that matter most to you. It can be a powerful way to bring together people who share your vision and can foster a strong, engaged network.

In essence, participating in online communities is about building a bridge to connect with others in meaningful ways. It's an opportunity to engage, learn, and share, turning the solitary act of remote work into a communal journey of shared growth and discovery. So dive in, contribute authentically, and you might find that these virtual spaces can make a real difference in your professional life.

# Chapter 9: Staying Productive on the Go

In the dynamic realm of remote work, flexibility is a valued ally. Whether you're catching a flight, sitting in a sunlit café, or working from a train station, maintaining productivity outside of your usual workspace can be challenging yet invigorating. The core of unlocking this potential lies in adapting to work while traveling and embracing portable tools and apps that cater to your needs.

First, consider the environments you'll find yourself in. Each setting brings its own distractions and opportunities. Being aware of these can help you make proactive choices. For example, background noise in a café can either fuel creativity or hamper concentration, depending on how you're wired. Adjusting your environment by using noise-canceling headphones or finding a quieter corner can make a significant difference.

**Adapting your mindset is crucial too.** Flexibility is at the heart of remote work, and it becomes even more vital when you're on the move. Though routines are important, don't be afraid to modify them to fit your new context. Traveling can disrupt traditional work patterns, but it also offers the chance to break monotony and refresh your creativity. Look for inspiration in new surroundings, allowing the change in scenery to bring fresh perspectives.

Next, leverage technology to keep your workflow smooth. Today's digital landscape is replete with apps and tools designed for mobile productivity. Cloud storage solutions ensure your work is accessible from any device, even if your primary laptop decides to take an unexpected break. Project management apps can help keep your team in sync, no matter where in the world they are. The key is to select tools that align with your style and work demands.

Ultimately, staying productive on the go requires a balance of preparation and adaptability. Equip yourself with the right tools, stay open to adjusting your routines, and embrace the possibilities that new settings offer. This approach ensures that no matter where your journey takes you, productivity remains within reach.

## Adapting to Work While Traveling

The allure of remote work isn't just about ditching the commute or working in your pajamas. It's about the freedom to take your work anywhere, from bustling coffee shops in Paris to serene beaches in Bali. Yet, as appealing as this sounds, working while traveling requires a strategic approach to maintain productivity. The key is to go beyond a romanticized vision of the nomadic lifestyle and focus on practical steps to adapt your work style to different environments.

Imagine starting your day in a foreign city, perhaps sipping a coffee in a street-side café. The change of scenery can be invigorating, but it can also present unique distractions. To tackle these, set a routine that mirrors what you have at home. Consistency can ground you amidst the novelty of new locations. When your environment constantly changes, having a stable daily structure provides a sense of normalcy, helping your mind transition smoothly between work and exploration.

Flexibility is equally important, though. While routines provide structure, travel often introduces unpredictable elements. Flights get delayed, accommodations change, and local events capture your attention. Embracing this unpredictability while maintaining a core schedule can help. Set aside specific blocks of time for work but allow flexibility within those blocks. Maybe you spend the morning working and the afternoon experiencing local culture, adjusting your priorities as needed.

For remote workers, ensuring connectivity is vital. A reliable internet connection is your lifeline. Before traveling, research your destination's connectivity options. Some cities offer free public WiFi, while others may have limited access. Consider investing in a mobile hotspot or a global SIM card as a backup. Staying connected isn't just about having internet; it's about maintaining the ability to connect with your team, access files, and meet deadlines anywhere you go.

Working across time zones adds another layer of complexity. When your team's 9-to-5 overlaps with your nighttime, align your workflows around overlapping hours and agree on core communication times. Use scheduling apps to keep track of different time zones. Prioritize tasks that require collaboration during these hours and save solo work for when you're offline. This ensures seamless communication while honoring both your team's requirements and your travel experiences.

Portable tools and apps are invaluable for adapting to work while traveling. Cloud storage services like Google Drive or Dropbox mean you can access your work from any device. Project management tools ensure you can update or assign tasks on the go. Keep your tech gear light but efficient: a compact laptop, noise-canceling headphones, and perhaps a tablet for flexibility. Each piece should serve a purpose and enhance your ability to work effectively from wherever you are.

Another crucial element of adapting to travel is managing expectations. Communication with your team or clients about your travel plans is essential to avoid misunderstandings. Inform them about your availability and potential internet issues in advance. This openness cultivates trust and understanding, ensuring they're onboard when faced with the occasional hiccup in communication or sudden plan changes.

Besides the logistical aspects, an adapting mindset is indispensable. Traveling exposes you to different cultures, perspectives, and work ethics. Embrace the local way of life and integrate it into your routine where possible. Balance work priorities with cultural immersion. Observing new customs and trying local delicacies can refresh your creativity, leading to more innovative ideas and solutions in your work.

Maintaining productivity while traveling is as much about mental stamina as it is about logistics. Focus on practices that support well-being, like regular exercise or meditation, which can help you adapt to new environments both physically and mentally. Short breaks to stretch or walk around can revitalize your productivity levels and help you tackle tasks with renewed energy.

Finally, learn as you go. Each travel experience is a chance to refine your remote working techniques. What worked flawlessly in one destination might require tweaks in another. Reflect on each trip. Did you find a perfect coffee shop with an excellent WiFi connection that enhances your productivity, or perhaps a particular time when you're most focused despite time zone differences? Use these insights to continually adapt and optimize your traveling work life.

Adapting to work while traveling is not just a challenge but a journey to discovering more flexible, resilient work practices. It's about finding balance and efficiency in diverse locations while drawing inspiration from these vibrant backdrops. This dynamic mode of working allows for not just a job you can do anywhere, but one that thrives anywhere. As you set off on your next journey, embrace the lifestyle as a catalyst for personal and professional growth.

## Portable Tools and Apps

In this digital age, staying productive on the go has evolved from a convenience to a necessity. Remote work demands adaptability and the right portable tools and apps can make all the difference. Imagine this: you're en route to a meeting or perhaps working from a quaint café in a city you've just explored. In such dynamic settings, having your digital toolkit at the ready is both empowering and liberating. These tools don't just enable work; they enhance how you manage your tasks, communication, and creativity no matter where you find yourself.

First things first—think of your smartphone as a Swiss Army knife for remote work. It's more than just a communication device; it's a gateway to a plethora of apps that keep your workflow seamless. Task management apps like *Todoist* or *Trello* allow you to organize tasks with intuitive drag-and-drop methods, prioritize your to-do list, and set deadlines while syncing across devices. This ensures you don't miss a beat, whether you're catching a flight or waiting for your next ride.

Seamless communication is another cornerstone of productivity. While emails serve their purpose, instant messaging platforms such as *Slack* or *Microsoft Teams* transform how you interact with your team on the move. Need to share files or need a quick video call? These apps have got you covered. Their integration capabilities mean you can connect them with your calendars and project management tools, creating a web of interconnected productivity resources.

For those who frequently engage in creative work or manage content, apps like *Adobe Creative Cloud* deliver immense flexibility. They offer mobile versions of robust software like Photoshop and Illustrator, allowing you to edit visuals or create stunning graphics without needing a desktop. And when inspiration strikes unexpectedly, being able to sketch or edit on-the-go can be a game-changer.

Another crucial aspect of portable work is document management. Gone are the days when physical paperwork was cumbersome. Cloud services like *Google Drive*, *Dropbox*, and *Box* ensure you have access to your documents wherever you are. These services allow for collaborative editing and are indispensable when you need to share large files rapidly. Additionally, their offline capabilities mean you're never hindered by lack of internet access.

If your work involves frequent travel, expense tracking apps like *Expensify* can save you considerable time and effort. These apps automate receipt tracking and mileage logging, making financial management straightforward and efficient. Likewise, booking tools such as *Kayak* or *Skyscanner* help plan your travels efficiently, ensuring you stay connected and productive without logistical hiccups.

A robust VPN app should be part of your digital arsenal to ensure security when accessing public Wi-Fi networks. Apps like *NordVPN* or *ExpressVPN* encrypt your data and protect your privacy, adding a necessary security layer in today's digital landscape.

Learning and development is another aspect where portable tools shine. Platforms such as *Coursera* or *LinkedIn Learning* can help you upskill at your own pace. They offer flexibility to download content for offline learning, letting you make productive use of commuting times or during flights when internet access could be restricted.

The modern remote worker's toolkit is as diverse as it is essential. All these apps and tools form a unique ecosystem, designed to foster productivity, streamline communication, and enhance collaboration, regardless of geographical location. The beauty of these portable tools lies in their adaptability; they not only accommodate the demands of remote work but also empower individuals by offering flexibility and independence.

This array of technologies is not set in stone—it's important to continuously evaluate and update your tools based on your evolving needs. With the rapidly changing technological landscape, new apps are constantly being developed, offering innovative solutions to remote work challenges. Embracing this change is not only wise but necessary for long-term productivity and effectiveness.

The journey toward mastering mobile productivity requires willingness and adaptability. By strategically selecting from this arsenal of tools, you're not solely enhancing your work; you're setting the stage for a richer, more connected professional journey—wherever it may lead. Let these tools be your trusted allies in navigating the exciting yet complex terrain of remote work.

# Chapter 10: Managing Remote Teams

Managing remote teams presents a unique set of challenges and opportunities. It's about more than just overseeing tasks and setting deadlines. It's about inspiring and guiding a group of individuals who, despite being miles apart, share a common goal. In the virtual space, managers must rely on trust and clear communication, often becoming the glue that holds the team together. Effective leadership in this realm requires a blend of empathy, adaptability, and vision.

**Communication** emerges as the cornerstone of successful remote team management. Clear, concise, and consistent communication can bridge the distance, allowing team members to feel connected and informed. This involves using the right digital tools to facilitate conversations, whether through video calls, team chats, or project management platforms. Regular check-ins, both group and one-on-one, help maintain engagement and provide insight into individual progress.

Leaders must embrace a culture of transparency and encourage feedback, fostering an environment where everyone feels heard. It's crucial to celebrate successes and recognize the efforts of your team, nurturing morale and motivation. Building a culture of accountability is another vital aspect. Clearly define roles and responsibilities, but balance these expectations with flexibility, understanding that team members are managing their productivity around unique personal circumstances.

An essential leadership skill in remote teams is the ability to measure progress quantitatively and qualitatively. While tracking key performance indicators can provide a snapshot of achievements, other factors such as creativity, problem-solving, and collaboration paint a fuller picture of a team's accomplishments. Managers should aim to create a balanced approach that appreciates both tangible results and the more subtle, yet equally important, contributions.

In the end, managing remote teams is an exercise in continuous learning and adaptation. The landscape is ever-evolving, and what worked yesterday might need tweaking tomorrow. By staying open to new strategies and maintaining a strong connection with your team, managers can navigate the complexities of remote work and emerge stronger and more united.

## Leadership Skills for Virtual Teams

In today's ever-evolving work environment, where remote and hybrid models are becoming the norm, the essence of leadership cannot be overstated. Traditional leadership skills get a new layer of complexity when applied to virtual teams. Leading in a virtual landscape means not only reaching your remote team's goals but also ensuring that every team member feels connected and valued. This section aims to outline key leadership skills that will empower you to leverage the full potential of a virtual team.

First and foremost, effective communication tops the leadership skills list. In a remote setting, where face-to-face interactions are limited, you have to rely heavily on digital communication tools. Mastering these tools goes beyond knowing how to use them. It involves crafting messages that are clear, engaging, and tailorable to different communication styles within your team. Successful leaders have a knack for reading between the virtual lines and picking up on the nuances of written communication, ensuring that no one feels disconnected or left out.

The second vital skill is emotional intelligence, especially empathy. Virtual teams can often feel like islands, with each member fending for themselves in their respective locations. As a leader, fostering genuine relationships is crucial. Be mindful of the silent cues and the unspoken words during video calls. Make an effort to understand individual challenges and offer support, whether it's through flexible working hours for someone managing family obligations or providing mental health resources. Empathetic leaders build trust and a sense of belonging, which are fundamental for any team to thrive.

Adaptability takes on new significance when managing a virtual team. The remote work landscape can change swiftly with technological advancements, shifts in client requirements, or global events. Being adaptable isn't just about weathering these changes, but proactively seeking out opportunities for innovation and improvement. Encourage your team to approach challenges with a growth mindset. When team members see their leader gracefully navigating the unpredictable, they feel more secure in taking calculated risks themselves.

Let's not ignore the importance of fostering autonomy. Micro-management can be stifling in a physical office, but in a virtual space, it's even more detrimental. It can erode trust and impede productivity. Effective leaders know how to empower their team by focusing on outcomes, not processes. Set clear objectives, provide the necessary resources, and then step back. Trust your team to achieve their goals. Celebrate initiative and ingenuity, which can fuel motivation and drive within the team.

Accountability and transparency go hand in hand and are indispensable in virtual leadership. In a digital space, it's easy for tasks and responsibilities to become muddied. To combat this, establish clear expectations from the start. Use project management tools that offer visibility to the whole team, allowing members to see what others are working on and how tasks align with collective objectives. When accountability is shared and understood, teams can work autonomously with confidence.

A great leader is also an advocate for continuous learning and professional development. The best virtual teams are those that are evolving. Encourage your team to take courses, attend webinars, or join virtual workshops. Highlight professional growth opportunities and be a mentor in helping them reach their career milestones. Adapt the team's goals to meet individual learning objectives, and you'll create an environment where personal and professional growth dovetail seamlessly.

Feedback loops are crucial in managing remote teams. Without casual office interactions, team members might be left in the dark about their performance or the impact of their contributions. Establish regular one-on-one check-ins and team meetings specifically for feedback sessions. Feedback should be a two-way street; promote dialogue, not monologue. When team members feel heard, they're more likely to embrace feedback and participate in crafting solutions.

Finally, celebrate your team's diversity, as virtual teams are often composed of members from varied backgrounds and cultures. Lean into this diversity by encouraging different perspectives and ideas. This diversity is a strength that can lead to richer discussions and more innovative solutions. Create an inclusive culture where everyone has a seat at the table, granted the opportunity to share their unique perspectives.

In summary, leading virtual teams effectively revolves around communication, empathy, adaptability, autonomy, accountability, continuous learning, feedback, and inclusivity. Mastering these skills can feel overwhelming, but remember that the most effective leaders didn't learn these overnight. Start small, stay consistent, and remain open to learning. As you enhance your leadership skills, you'll discover new ways to connect with and empower your team, no matter where each of you is located.

## Tracking Progress and Accountability

In the realm of remote work, overseeing a team's progress and ensuring accountability often feels like walking a tightrope. It's a delicate balance; too loose, and things fall apart, too strict, and creativity suffocates. How do you walk this line? The answer lies in blending structure with flexibility, anchoring processes with empathy. Both you and your team must feel engaged, not just tasked.

The heart of tracking is setting clear expectations. Without a shared understanding of what success looks like, it's like playing a game without knowing the rules. Goals should be SMART—specific, measurable, achievable, relevant, and time-bound. This ensures everyone is pulling in the same direction, regardless of where they are in the world. It's not about micromanaging every detail but focusing on outcomes. Think about it this way: it's less about the hours clocked and more about the value delivered.

Modern tools are the great enablers in this process. Platforms like Trello, Asana, or Monday.com offer visual ways to manage tasks and monitor progress. They create a shared space where every team member can see the roadmap, mark milestones, and adjust workloads. Transparency fosters accountability. When team members understand how their work contributes to the bigger picture, they naturally feel more responsible and invested.

But remember, tools are but instruments—they can't replace the human touch. Regular check-ins, whether through video calls or messaging apps, are essential in maintaining a connection. These sessions shouldn't feel like interrogations but rather opportunities for dialogue and development. Ask guiding questions, like, "What's on your priority list this week?" or "How can I support you better?" This communicates trust and fosters an environment where team members can openly discuss challenges and achievements.

Accountability also comes from tracking not just *what* was done, but *how* it was done. Did the process enhance team morale, foster collaboration, or was it a solo grind? Reflecting on these qualitative aspects helps fine-tune workflows and ensures that team dynamics are strengthening rather than being eroded by distance. After all, remote success is as much about culture as it is about completing tasks.

It's crucial to celebrate wins, both big and small. Recognition breeds motivation. Whether it's a shoutout in a team meeting, a detailed email, or even a simple 'thanks' in a chat, acknowledgment goes a long way. In a remote setting where spontaneous office high-fives aren't feasible, deliberate acts of appreciation become even more important. They remind people of their value and the value of their contributions.

Technology is evolving, and with it, our means to manage remote teams. The use of artificial intelligence and automated analytics can offer insights into work patterns and productivity levels without infringing on privacy. For instance, AI tools can suggest when a team member might be overloaded based on workload patterns and historical data. This allows managers to intervene with support rather than sanction, reinforcing a caring and supportive work culture.

Of course, accountability is a two-way street. Just as team members are accountable for their tasks, leaders must be accountable for providing direction, resources, and support. This means being available, offering constructive feedback, and being open to feedback in return. Practicing what you preach in terms of accountability encourages reciprocal behavior and builds trust across the team.

Consider implementing feedback loops as part of your process. This could involve monthly performance reviews or even informal one-on-ones to gauge satisfaction and areas for improvement. Remember, feedback is not only about critique but also about appreciation and learning. It's a chance to reinforce team goals, align priorities, and strengthen bonds.

To cultivate a habit of self-accountability within the team, encourage a culture of reflection. Encourage team members to reflect on their weekly achievements and challenges. This reflective practice nudges individuals to take ownership of their work, identifying where they might need help or where they excelled. Personal accountability enhances team accountability, resulting in a more resilient and robust organizational structure.

In summary, tracking progress and maintaining accountability in remote teams require a multifaceted approach. It's about utilizing the right tools and technologies while embedding empathy and recognition in leadership practices. By fostering a culture of clarity, communication, and celebration, you can drive a team that is not only productive but also cohesive and content. In such an environment, accountability naturally follows, emerging as a shared value rather than an imposed rule.

# Chapter 11: The Nomadic Lifestyle

Imagine waking up to the sound of ocean waves in Bali one month, and then exploring the bustling streets of Tokyo the next. The digital nomad lifestyle embodies a modern-day freedom that many remote workers dream of. It's a blend of work and adventure, offering an unprecedented level of flexibility. Yet, embracing this lifestyle requires more than just packing a laptop and hitting the road. It involves a mindful approach to balance and adaptability, crucial for sustaining productivity while relishing the journey.

At its core, the nomadic lifestyle is about making deliberate choices that align with both professional goals and personal passions. It's about crafting a life that's not confined to a singular locale. Successful digital nomads master the art of planning—selecting destinations that support both work and leisure. Whether it's leveraging coworking spaces or tapping into local communities, setting up a 'home base' in each new location becomes an essential skill. Embracing change, they learn to find comfort in uncertainty, using it as fuel for innovation and growth.

The stories of seasoned digital nomads provide a wealth of inspiration and practical advice. Take Lisa, a graphic designer who carries her workspace in a backpack. Her story isn't just about working from dream destinations—it's about the determination to build a business on her own terms. For Lisa, each city she visits becomes a new chapter in her life and work, filled with cultural insights that influence her creativity and productivity. Her approach to challenges isn't about avoidance—it's about cultivating resilience and viewing obstacles as opportunities.

A nomadic lifestyle isn't devoid of hurdles. Connectivity issues, time zone adjustments, and periodic bouts of loneliness are all part of the journey. However, with the right mindset and tools, these challenges can be managed effectively. Embracing the freedom and adventure of a location-independent lifestyle can lead to a richer, more fulfilling work experience, blending the best of productivity and exploration.

## Embracing the Freedom of Remote Work

The nomadic lifestyle offers a tantalizing promise: the freedom to work from anywhere, with horizons that stretch as far as the imagination can wander. But what does it truly mean to embrace this freedom? At its core, it's about breaking the chains of traditional office constraints while crafting a professional life that aligns with personal aspirations and desires.

Once shackled by the limitations of geography, individuals are now exploring opportunities that were previously unimaginable. Imagine sipping coffee at a café nestled in the Parisian streets while closing deals with clients halfway across the world. This isn't just a dream; it's a new reality that remote work affords. This newfound freedom allows remote workers to rediscover what truly matters—whether it's spending more time with family, cultivating passions, or simply enjoying the morning sun from a different corner of the globe.

Despite its appeal, this lifestyle demands a shift in mindset, one where adaptability becomes a valued trait. Remote workers must hone the ability to adjust quickly to diverse environments, each offering unique challenges and lessons. Flexibility and resourcefulness become second nature, as the journey doesn't always follow a prescribed path. Each day unfolds with spontaneity, bringing moments that infuse ordinary routines with extraordinary experiences.

As workers settle into this rhythm, they discover a profound sense of empowerment. Choosing a workspace that kindles creativity and productivity empowers them to balance life and work seamlessly, on their own terms. The autonomy to design a unique daily schedule, free from the rigidity of 9-to-5 constraints, enhances both professional fulfillment and personal well-being. It's about creating a harmonious balance where professional efficiency meets personal satisfaction.

The benefits of this lifestyle are undeniably alluring. Yet, diving headfirst into the realm of remote work isn't without challenges. The absence of a structured office environment requires self-discipline and initiative. Without traditional oversight, accountability rests solely on the individual's shoulders. Developing effective habits becomes crucial to ensuring productivity, as does maintaining motivation amidst ever-changing settings.

With freedom comes the responsibility of setting boundaries. It's easy to blur the lines between work and leisure when the boundaries themselves are fluid. Finding this balance is essential for fostering a sustainable relationship between personal and professional life. Setting clear priorities and delineating work hours can help protect both mental health and job performance.

For those embarking on this journey, cultivating a sense of connection is vital. Community doesn't dissipate with distance; rather, it evolves. Thanks to digital platforms, remote workers can connect instantly, building networks and forming virtual communities with like-minded individuals across continents. These connections—though virtual—prove invaluable in sharing insights, experiences, and even comfort during times of solitude.

Remote work strips away traditional hierarchies, encouraging collaboration based on merit and skill rather than proximity or position. This fosters a sense of equity and camaraderie among teams spread worldwide. Embracing this democratic shift can lead to innovative ideas and collaborations that transcend geographical barriers.

While the flexibility of remote work can enhance work-life balance, it also offers the opportunity to weave personal growth into the professional journey. It presents the freedom to explore skills and interests, allowing time to engage in learning and self-improvement ventures that may have seemed out of reach in conventional settings. This dual pursuit of career and personal development enriches the remote worker's professional path.

Being part of this ever-expanding nomadic workforce can also inspire others within one's circle. It sets a precedent for what's possible, challenging the status quo and encouraging the pursuit of fulfilling, adaptable careers. Witnessing the success and balance achieved by remote workers can motivate colleagues, friends, and family to rethink traditional work norms and explore the viability of pursuing their passions alongside their careers.

It's important to acknowledge that this lifestyle isn't a one-size-fits-all solution. Each individual must weigh the pros and cons, assess their own circumstances and decide if the remote route aligns with their personal and professional goals. Depth and richness in experiences will vary, depending on how one chooses to navigate the seas of remote work.

Indeed, embracing the freedom of remote work isn't merely about changing locations; it's about transforming the way we view and engage with work itself. As remote work continues to redefine norms, it's reshaping more than just the office walls—it's creating a future where work is truly integrated into the tapestry of life, allowing anyone to live and work with intention, independence, and infinite possibility.

All it takes is the courage to leap into the unknown, a willingness to embrace change, and the determination to forge a path that is uniquely one's own. Remote work, when embraced fully, can be a powerful tool for crafting a life that resonates with both purpose and passion. The opportunities are vast, the potential limitless, and the freedom, indeed, captivating.

## Stories from Successful Digital Nomads

Embracing the nomadic lifestyle isn't just an escape from the cubicle; it's a vibrant journey that resonates with freedom, adaptability, and personal growth. Across the globe, a breed of ambitious and adventurous individuals is making this lifestyle work seamlessly, crafting unique stories that serve as a beacon for aspiring digital nomads. Each story reveals a tapestry of experiences—from vibrant cultures to unexpected challenges—that fuel the passion for a life untethered from conventional workspaces.

Meet Alex, a skilled web designer who traded the monotony of a 9-to-5 for the excitement of perpetual movement. Originally from San Francisco, Alex decided to take his career on the road, setting his sights on the dynamic coworking communities of Southeast Asia. "I wanted more than just travel; I wanted to immerse myself in new cultures," he explains. Alex's journey began in Bali, where he found not only stunning beaches but also a thriving community of like-minded individuals eager to share experiences and collaborate. His productivity soared as he balanced work with adventure—coding from a surfside café one day and brainstorming with fellow nomads at a local meetup the next.

Then there's Jessica, a social media strategist who thrives on flexibility and exploration. After a decade in the corporate hustle, Jessica embraced the digital nomad lifestyle in pursuit of learning and growth. "The world became my source of inspiration," she notes. From the cobblestone streets of Lisbon to the bustling markets of Bangkok, Jessica discovered the creative pulse that different cultures offered. Remote work allowed her the luxury to choose her office view each day, transforming mundane tasks into opportunities for creativity and innovation. For her, the secret was setting clear boundaries between work and play, integrating local traditions into her routine to enrich both her personal and professional life.

In contrast, we have David, a software developer who exchanged his New York apartment for a campervan, embracing the call of the open road. "I needed space not just physically but mentally," David shares. The decision to embark on a journey across the United States was driven by a need for personal reflection and growth. Working from national parks and routine pit stops in small towns provided a unique perspective on work-life balance. Challenges such as fluctuating internet connectivity were met with resilience and ingenuity, leading David to innovate solutions involving satellite connections and offline productivity tools. His story underscores the importance of adaptability and the rewarding serenity found in slower-paced surroundings.

Meanwhile, we can't overlook the story of Mia and Liam, a couple running an online educational portal for language learners. They embarked on a global journey to enrich both their knowledge and that of their students by living in the countries of the languages they were teaching. "Our passion for languages and cultures could finally be shared in a way textbooks couldn't convey," Mia reveals. Their adventure provided a unique chance to test educational content in real-time cultural contexts, making learning more dynamic and engaging for their audience. The duo emphasizes the significance of nurturing connections, both professional and personal, as they travel. By networking with local educators and participating in cultural exchange programs, they enriched their curriculum and fueled their business with authenticity and depth.

No digital nomad story is complete without discussing the entrepreneurial spirit of individuals like Ben, an e-commerce consultant who harnessed the power of remote work to tap into emerging markets. Relocating to Eastern Europe was both strategic and spontaneous. "I wanted to immerse myself in places with untapped potential," he explains. The lower cost of living allowed Ben to invest more into his venture, offering bespoke consultancy services to startups. Immersing himself in local entrepreneurship scenes opened new avenues for collaboration and innovation, reinforcing his belief that every place, no matter how remote, has a story to tell and a market to explore.

Another compelling narrative is of Sarai, a yoga instructor who transformed her passion into a globally accessible digital service. Recognizing the global demand for wellness, Sarai developed an online platform to conduct virtual classes. Her travels took her from wellness retreats in Costa Rica to serene Japanese Zen gardens, infusing her sessions with the wisdom and tranquility of diverse practices. Sarai's journey is a testament to the positive impact of remote work on personal well-being and professional fulfillment. Her motto, "Stay grounded while exploring the clouds," resonates with those seeking balance between the freedom of travel and the discipline of a work routine.

Finally, the experiences of these digital nomads reveal a universal truth: that the world is full of possibilities for those willing to step beyond traditional boundaries. Their stories are not just about triumphing over geographical challenges but also about redefining success, community, and creativity. They remind us that the landscapes we choose to work from deeply influence our mindset and productivity, and that with the right tools and vision, any corner of the world can become the nucleus of professional and personal evolution.

These voices showcase resilience, innovation, and the profound satisfaction found at the confluence of work and adventure. As we draw inspiration from these narratives, it's clear that the digital nomad lifestyle offers more than just a passport to work globally—it's a path to personal growth and global connection. For remote workers everywhere, these stories are a call to embrace the opportunities that freedom and technology afford, pursuing not just a career, but a life filled with enriching experiences and endless possibilities.

# Chapter 12: Handling Work Challenges Remotely

Remote work offers unparalleled flexibility, but it's not without its challenges. Navigating these obstacles requires resilience, creativity, and a proactive mindset. One of the biggest hurdles is remote work loneliness. The seclusion of working from home can amplify feelings of isolation, making it crucial to foster connectivity through virtual communities. While the lack of physical office dynamics can lead to disconnection, prioritizing regular virtual meetings and casual check-ins can invigorate the sense of belonging and camaraderie.

Technological issues also often loom large over remote work environments. A sudden disruption in internet connectivity or malfunctioning software can halt productivity abruptly. Thus, creating contingency plans and familiarizing oneself with alternative tools is essential. Equip yourself with a basic toolkit for troubleshooting common tech problems, and don't hesitate to reach out to technical support when needed. It's about being equipped and resilient in the face of digital disruptions.

Balancing these elements isn't just about minimizing the issues; it's about turning them into growth opportunities. Embrace downtime caused by technological hiccups to engage in upskilling or delve into creative brainstorming sessions. This mindset shift from obstacles to opportunities can significantly enhance personal and professional growth.

Finally, adaptability is key. Remote work demands an ability to navigate the unexpected and pivot quickly. Cultivating this adaptability helps you maintain momentum and ensures you're prepared for whatever comes your way. Embrace change, acknowledge challenges, and keep pressing forward. In the grand tapestry of remote work, each challenge is a thread contributing to the broader story of remote resilience and success.

## Navigating Remote Work Loneliness

As the world of work shifts increasingly onto digital platforms, many remote workers face a new and unanticipated challenge: loneliness. This isn't just a superficial lack of social interaction but a deeper feeling that can impact productivity and mental health. The good news? With awareness and proactive strategies, it's possible to mitigate these feelings and thrive in a remote work environment.

Isolation in remote work often stems from missing out on those everyday face-to-face interactions in an office setting, such as casual water cooler conversations or spontaneous collaboration sessions. These encounters, though sometimes overlooked, play a critical role in building a sense of community and belonging. When working from home or a different location entirely, this social void can exacerbate feelings of loneliness.

The first step in addressing remote work loneliness is acknowledging its existence. Many remote workers may not even realize they're experiencing loneliness until it begins to affect their mood or work output. It's important to recognize the signs early—feeling disengaged, struggling to concentrate, or even physical symptoms like headaches can all be linked to a lack of social interaction.

Creating a structured daily routine that includes scheduled social interactions can be incredibly helpful. While it might be tempting to coast through the day without much contact, setting up regular check-ins with colleagues or industry peers can provide much-needed interaction. These don't have to be lengthy meetings—short, focused conversations can have a significant impact on how connected you feel.

Engaging in virtual co-working sessions is another effective tactic. These sessions can make the virtual work landscape feel less like an isolated experience. Platforms offering communal virtual spaces or "working together" video calls can simulate the office atmosphere. By merely having others visible or audible as you work, you can recreate the ambiance of a shared workspace.

In addition to professional interactions, don't underestimate the power of non-work-related communication. Join interest groups or hobby clubs that meet online. These communities can provide emotional support and camaraderie, helping to balance the work-focused interactions with personal engagement and fulfillment.

Managers and team leaders play a vital role in curbing remote work loneliness. Encouraging open communication and regularly checking in with team members can create an environment where employees feel valued and included. Designing team-building activities that are actually enjoyable can also bolster a sense of unity within remotely distributed teams.

For those new to remote work, mentorship programs can serve as a lifeline. Connecting newcomers with more experienced remote workers can help them navigate the nuances of this work style while also providing them an immediate social connection within the organization. These bonds often lead to enriching professional growth and reduced feelings of isolation.

Maintaining a healthy work-life balance is crucial. Over-working can exacerbate loneliness as it might prevent you from engaging in offline social activities. Set strict boundaries for ending your workday and make time for social interests or physical activities outside your home. This deliberate balance helps differentiate work time from personal time, keeping loneliness at bay.

Sometimes, the loneliness stems not from the lack of interaction but rather from the nature of remote work itself, which can make us question our purpose and contribution. Take time to reflect on your work's impact and set personal and professional goals that drive motivation and satisfaction. Recognition, even self-acknowledgment of small victories and progress, can enhance the sense of purpose and connectivity to your role.

Given the pervasive use of technology in remote work, leveraging artificial intelligence and other tools can help streamline interactions that might otherwise feel multi-layered and fragmented. Utilizing smart scheduling apps, for instance, can organize virtual meet-ups efficiently, leaving more time for meaningful conversations.

Lastly, if loneliness becomes overwhelming, seeking professional support from a counselor or therapist should not be stigmatized. It's a responsible and proactive step toward maintaining mental health, allowing you to equip yourself with coping strategies tailored to your unique situation.

Remote work isn't just the way of the future; it's the present for many. By taking conscious steps to combat loneliness, remote workers can not just survive but thrive, enjoying all the benefits that come with a flexible and dynamic work environment. Together, with intention and community, we can embrace the potential of remote work while keeping human connection at its core.

## Dealing with Technological Issues

In the modern world of remote work, technology serves as both a bridge and a barrier. It's this double-edged sword that can connect you to colleagues across the globe in an instant yet leave you scrambling when a single device malfunctions. To thrive, remote workers must not only rely on technology but master it to ensure seamless productivity. This section explores the tools, strategies, and mindset required to tackle technological hurdles head-on, so you can focus on what truly matters: producing great work from anywhere.

When you're working remotely, technology is your lifeline. However, it's all too common for devices or software to fail at the most inopportune times. The first step in mitigating these issues is ensuring that you're using the right tools. Start with your primary device, whether it's a laptop or desktop, and keep it well-maintained. Regular updates and scheduled check-ups can prevent unexpected disruptions. You can avoid a lot of trouble later by setting these habits early on.

Another cornerstone of a robust remote work setup is a strong internet connection. It's vital to invest in high-speed internet and have a backup plan in place. Mobile hotspots or a secondary network can safeguard your connectivity against outages. Moreover, being mindful of the bandwidth consumed by your tasks can help prevent slowdowns during critical meetings or when submitting assignments.

Even with the best tools, you may encounter unexpected glitches. That's why it's important to have a set routine for troubleshooting. Familiarize yourself with common problems and quick fixes to resolve issues without losing precious time and mental energy. Online forums and tech support can be valuable resources but knowing your own system helps. By developing your troubleshooting skills, you enhance your ability to remain calm and composed when technological hiccups arise.

Besides hardware and software glitches, security poses a significant challenge in remote work scenarios. A security breach can disrupt your workflow and jeopardize sensitive information, so taking proactive steps to safeguard your digital environment is crucial. Regularly updating passwords and using two-factor authentication are simple yet effective practices to bolster your defenses.

In some cases, remote work can lead to tech overload, where the sheer volume of tools and platforms becomes overwhelming. If this happens, it might be time to audit your tech stack. Evaluate the necessity and efficiency of each tool you use. Simplification can do wonders for your workflow, and sometimes less truly is more. Eliminating unnecessary software not only streamlines processes but also reduces potential failure points.

Understanding your software suite is just as important as maintaining your hardware. Learning and mastering the various digital tools you work with can greatly enhance productivity and mitigate downtime caused by tech issues. Whether it's project management software, video conferencing tools, or collaboration platforms, investing time in training can pay dividends. Online courses or tutorials can often fill knowledge gaps efficiently.

Let's not forget the human aspect of technology use—communicating and collaborating effectively in a digital space can be as challenging as the tech issues themselves. Creating a protocol for seamless digital communication ensures that technical disruptions don't derail entire team initiatives. Clear guidelines about which platforms are for meeting, sharing files, or simple chats can prevent confusion and tech traffic jams.

The key to dealing with technological issues isn't just in the tools and practices adopted but also in the mindset you bring to work. Embracing a proactive, solution-oriented approach can make all the difference. With a positive attitude, you can view tech challenges as opportunities to learn and improve your digital resilience. Cultivating patience and adaptability not only helps you handle tech issues as they arise but also ensures you're ready for the next unknown hurdle.

However, there are times when technology fails us no matter how prepared we are. That's when support systems are invaluable. Establishing connections with IT professionals or tech-savvy colleagues can be a lifesaver. Having a tech buddy to consult in times of crisis can ease the stress of dealing with complex issues on your own. Even virtual check-in sessions with peers to exchange tips can provide insights into solutions you might never have considered.

Finally, take time to reflect on tech problems you encounter and how you address them. Regular self-evaluation can uncover areas for improvement or spotlight strategies that work well, guiding future efforts and reducing anxiety over technology hiccups. By fostering an environment that encourages continuous learning and adaptation, you can transform technological challenges from obstacles into stepping stones on your pathway to success.

In summary, dealing with technological issues as a remote worker means staying prepped, staying resilient, and staying connected. By understanding your tools, setting up safeguards, and maintaining a solution-focused attitude, you arm yourself to tackle tech troubles head-on, minimizing their impact on your work. Engage with technology as a partner rather than a hindrance, and watch as remote work becomes not only manageable but also profoundly rewarding.

# Chapter 13: Financial Management for Remote Workers

In today's ever-evolving digital landscape, managing one's finances effectively has become crucial for remote workers. The freedom and flexibility of remote work come with financial unpredictability, demanding a proactive approach. Embracing this mindset starts with acknowledging that income streams may fluctuate, especially for freelancers and independent contractors. By anticipating these fluctuations, remote workers can create a financial buffer that offers peace of mind and stability in the face of uncertainty.

While budgeting isn't the most thrilling task, it's undeniably powerful. It can transform financial chaos into clarity. Remote workers should prioritize setting clear financial goals and track their spending meticulously. A tip: categorize your expenses into fixed and variable costs. This distinction aids in identifying where potential savings can be made. Utilize digital tools and apps to monitor budgets regularly. With numerous options available, finding one that suits your lifestyle can make this process both manageable and even enjoyable.

Tax obligations can often seem daunting, especially when working remotely across different states or countries. Therefore, comprehending the tax implications of remote work should never be underestimated. Seek advice from a tax professional familiar with international and remote work circumstances to ensure you're compliant with all tax laws. It's vital to stay organized, keeping records of all business-related activities and expenses, which can be indispensable during tax season.

An often overlooked aspect of financial management for remote workers is saving for the future. Contributing to a retirement plan and building an emergency fund can provide a safety net for unforeseen challenges. Remember, no matter where you work, securing your financial future is a universal necessity. By mastering these financial management strategies, remote workers can not only survive but also thrive, finding success and satisfaction in their unique work environments.

## Budgeting for Variable Income

Managing your finances as a remote worker often feels like navigating a ship through turbulent seas. The unpredictable nature of variable income can be both thrilling and nerve-wracking. Whether you're a freelancer negotiating new projects, or a remote worker juggling multiple gigs, the key to financial stability lies in mastering the art of budgeting. Variable income isn't just a challenge; it's an opportunity to refine your financial prowess and embrace a lifestyle that thrives on flexibility and adaptability.

First, let's dive into the fundamental principle of budgeting for those with irregular income: understanding your monthly cash flow. Start by tracking all sources of income over several months to recognize a pattern or average earning. Analyzing past income helps set a realistic baseline and reduce the emotional rollercoaster that comes with variable paychecks. This baseline doesn't only prepare you for leaner months, it also offers peace of mind when your income surpasses expectations.

Building a robust emergency fund is, without question, a foundational step for remote workers. Ideally, this fund should cover three to six months' worth of living expenses, providing a buffer during slow periods or unexpected expenses. While it might feel daunting to stash away such a safety net, remember that even small, consistent contributions will accumulate over time. Regularly setting aside a portion of your income, regardless of its size, creates a cushion that shields you from falling into financial uncertainty.

Next, consider implementing a priority-based budgeting system. This involves categorizing your expenses into non-negotiable needs and flexible wants. Non-negotiable needs include rent, utilities, food, and essential insurance. Flexible wants, such as dining out or subscription services, can be adjusted based on your income fluctuations. Embracing this method ensures that your primary expenses are met while maintaining the freedom to enjoy life's luxuries during more profitable months.

Adopting the 50/30/20 rule is another effective strategy for managing variable income. Of course, the percentages might shift slightly based on individual circumstances, but this rule provides a solid framework. Allocate 50% of your income to needs, 30% to wants, and 20% to savings or debt repayment. When income grows, increase the allocation to savings and debt pay-off; when it shrinks, cut back on wants. This flexibility keeps your financial goals on track without sacrificing essential needs.

One distinct advantage of remote work is the potential to minimize certain expenses. Commuting costs, professional attire, and daily meals out can quickly add up; working remotely often eliminates these. Take advantage of this by allocating what you save in these areas to your savings or investment accounts. Over time, even minor adjustments can accumulate substantial long-term savings, contributing to financial security.

Consider setting up multiple bank accounts to compartmentalize your finances effectively. At the minimum, maintain separate accounts for income, expenses, and savings. This approach brings clarity to your financial picture, simplifies budgeting, and makes tracking where your money is going easier. Designating these different accounts also reduces the temptation to dip into savings when income is slow.

Leveraging technology can further streamline budgeting for remote workers. Numerous apps and digital tools are designed specifically to track irregular income and manage expenses effortlessly. Tools like Mint, YNAB, or QuickBooks give you insights into spending patterns and help automate the budgeting process. Utilizing such platforms can turn financial management into a seamless part of your routine rather than a monthly chore.

Harness the power of foresight. Anticipating potential income slumps allows you to adjust your budget proactively. If you know certain months tend to bring fewer projects or work opportunities, prepare by saving more in the preceding months or lining up additional income streams. Embracing a mindset of adaptability and forward-thinking converts potential financial challenges into foreseeable, manageable events.

Another aspect of budgeting for remote workers involves accounting for fluctuating tax obligations. As a freelancer or contract worker, taxes may not automatically be deducted from your earnings. Ensuring you set aside a portion of your income for taxes is crucial, potentially eliminating a future financial burden. Scheduling quarterly estimated tax payments is one way to smooth out cash flow and minimize the impact of annual taxes.

Diversifying your income streams presents a robust safeguard against the unpredictability of variable income. Balancing multiple projects, or even exploring passive income opportunities, spreads financial risk and boosts resilience. Remote work naturally opens doors to diverse income opportunities, making it easier than ever to pursue varied interests and professions without geographical limitations.

While focusing on financial literacy and sound budgeting practices is critical, it's equally important to remain compassionate with yourself through the ups and downs of irregular income. Financial stress is a potent productivity killer, and managing money should not come at the cost of mental well-being. Employing practices such as mindfulness, seeking professional financial advice, or connecting with online communities of remote workers can provide support and a sense of solidarity.

In the end, budgeting for variable income isn't merely a skill—it's a pathway toward personal development and financial independence. It requires awareness, assessment, and adjustment to navigate the flux of the freelance and remote work landscape. With thoughtful planning and the right strategies, remote workers can wield variable income as a tool to not only sustain their lifestyles but enrich them, paving the way for a future that's as secure as it is exciting.

## Tax Considerations

Stepping into the world of remote work reveals a landscape filled with flexibility and freedom, but it also ushers in complexities that require attention, especially when it comes to taxes. Whether you're a freelancer, contractor, or a full-time remote employee, understanding your tax obligations is crucial. It's not just about compliance; it's about optimizing your financial situation and avoiding unnecessary stress. Let's explore how to navigate these waters with confidence.

First, let's consider the basic principles. Remote work often involves receiving income from different states or even countries, which can complicate your tax situation. Unlike office-based employees who have a clear tax jurisdiction, remote workers might find themselves juggling multiple tax rules. Knowing where your income is sourced is the starting point. Are you working in the state where your employer is based, or are you living in a different state? Each scenario can lead to different tax implications, and it's crucial to identify them early on.

For those working across state lines within the United States, understanding the concept of 'state income tax nexus' is important. Nexus determines whether a state has the legal authority to tax you. Many states expect taxes if you are physically present and working there regularly. Meanwhile, some states have reciprocal tax agreements, which allow you to work in one state but pay taxes in another where you live. Knowing these distinctions can save you from double taxation.

International remote workers face an even more elaborate tax maze. If you're working for a company based in another country or taking freelance projects globally, you might need to consider foreign income taxes. Many countries require tax filings if you exceed a certain threshold of income within their borders. However, tools like tax treaties and the Foreign Earned Income Exclusion can help mitigate potential double taxation. Familiarizing yourself with these provisions can significantly reduce your tax burden.

Furthermore, remote work often means taking on dual roles as both employee and entrepreneur. As a freelancer or independent contractor, you're responsible for self-employment taxes, which cover social security and Medicare. This includes both the employee and employer portion, effectively doubling your contribution. Understanding this and planning for it can prevent unpleasant surprises come tax season. It's wise to allocate around 25-30% of your income to cover these taxes.

Tracking expenses is another essential practice for remote workers. Many work-related expenses can be deducted from your taxable income, reducing your overall tax bill. If you maintain a dedicated home office space, you might qualify for a home office deduction. This includes rent, utilities, internet bills, and office supplies, among others – but they need to meet specific criteria set by the IRS. Regularly updating and organizing these expenses can make the deduction process straightforward and more beneficial.

Despite these opportunities, the IRS has specific rules regarding what qualifies for deductions. Your home office must be a dedicated space used exclusively for your work, not just a corner of your living room. On top of that, your income must align with the deductions claimed; excessive deductions compared to income can trigger audits. Being diligent and honest in your bookkeeping ensures you're benefitting legally and ethically.

The use of technology in remote work introduces unique tax considerations as well. Subscriptions to essential software, digital tools, and even certain tech gadgets can be considered deductible expenses if they're used extensively for work purposes. Paying for platforms that facilitate your productivity or connectivity, like video conferencing tools and project management software, are often reasonable deductions. Keep a detailed record of these receipts and justify their proportional use for work to maximize your deductible amount.

Engaging a tax professional, especially one proficient in remote work tax scenarios, can prove invaluable. They can provide insights on optimizing deductions, navigating multi-state or international tax laws, and ensuring complete compliance with tax regulations. Investing in professional advice can yield substantial savings and peace of mind, allowing you to focus on your work rather than looming tax deadlines.

For many remote workers, estimating quarterly taxes is another vital aspect. Unlike traditional employment, taxes aren't withheld from your income. You're required to pay estimated taxes quarterly to avoid penalties. Calculating these can be daunting, especially with fluctuating freelance income. Utilizing tax software or consulting with a financial advisor can streamline the process, aiding you in staying on top of your obligations without overpayment.

Finally, legislative changes occur frequently, impacting tax obligations. Staying informed about recent tax law changes, especially those influenced by shifts towards remote work, is vital. Engaging with professional communities or tax forums can provide up-to-date information and tailored advice, directly affecting your approach to financial management.

Embracing remote work invites not just a new way of working but a new approach to handling financial responsibilities. By understanding and organizing your tax considerations, you gain financial clarity. This empowers you to focus on what truly matters – thriving in your remote work lifestyle, unburdened by the complexities that taxes often present.

# Chapter 14: Personal Development and Learning

In the ever-evolving landscape of remote work, prioritizing personal development isn't just beneficial—it's essential. Embracing continuous learning fuels innovation and adaptability, traits that are indispensable when change is the only constant. For remote workers, freelancers, and managers, actively engaging in personal development means remaining relevant and competitive in an increasingly global market. This chapter explores how to weave learning into the fabric of your daily routine seamlessly.

Opportunities for online learning are more abundant than ever. Whether it's honing a new skill or deepening existing expertise, resources like MOOCs, podcasts, webinars, and virtual workshops abound. The key is to remain curious and proactive. Leverage platforms like Coursera, LinkedIn Learning, or Udemy, which offer a plethora of courses that fit various interests and skill levels. Not only do these platforms provide flexibility, allowing learners to set their own pace, but they also offer connectivity—placing individuals in virtual classrooms with peers worldwide.

Balancing skill development with work involves strategic planning and discipline. It starts with assessing your career goals and identifying the skills required to achieve them. Once you have clarity, create a personalized learning plan that aligns with your work schedule. Remember, consistency is more crucial than the time spent. Even dedicating twenty minutes a day to focused learning can lead to substantial progress over time. Incorporating learning into your routine not only prevents stagnation but also stimulates your mind, which can lead to increased productivity in your work responsibilities.

Never underestimate the power of reflection and feedback as tools for growth. After completing a learning module or book, take a moment to reflect on how the new knowledge applies to your role or can enhance your work. Seek feedback from mentors, peers, or online communities to gain diverse perspectives. Constructive criticism can offer invaluable insights, paving the way for further development.

Moreover, personal development shouldn't be an isolated endeavor. Engage with communities that share your learning journeys. Whether through social media groups, local meetups, or collaborative online platforms, connecting with others can offer support, accountability, and shared knowledge. Networking with peers going through similar challenges and successes enriches the learning experience and often leads to unforeseen opportunities.

In conclusion, personal development and learning are not mere add-ons to remote work—they're integral components of a thriving, sustainable career. Embrace the diverse resources available, integrate learning systematically into your routines, and leverage the power of community engagement. Through thoughtful planning and dedication, you can transform personal growth from a lofty goal into a tangible reality that enhances both your professional and personal life in the dynamic world of remote work.

## Opportunities for Online Learning

In the dynamic landscape of remote work, personal growth and continual learning aren't just beneficial—they're essential. The digital age has flung open the doors to a wealth of online learning opportunities that can enhance your skills, broaden your horizons, and elevate your professional game. When you're working from a remote setting, the challenge lies in ensuring these opportunities align with your personal and professional goals.

The beauty of online learning lies in its flexibility. Whether you want to master a new software, learn coding, or understand the latest trends in digital marketing, there are courses tailored to just about every interest and need. Platforms like Coursera, Udacity, and edX offer a plethora of courses ranging from quick-start mini-courses to professional certifications and even degrees. You can craft your educational journey around your schedule, allowing you to pace your learning according to your workload and personal commitments.

What's more thrilling is the scope of these platforms to connect you with experts and learners globally. Imagine participating in a business strategy class facilitated by a top professor from an Ivy League school, all from the comfort of your makeshift kitchen office. These interactions can lead to enlightening discussions, innovative ideas, and maybe even friendships with like-minded professionals, all without leaving your home.

Furthermore, on-demand learning breaks the mold of traditional education. Gone are the rigid lecture times and droning instructors. Instead, you engage with immersive content through videos, interactive assignments, and peer feedback. This setup fosters a personalized learning environment where you control the when, how, and what of your educational path. It's like having a customizable toolkit, ready to sharpen your skills as and when you see fit.

Yet, the abundance of resources can also be daunting. It can become easy to sign up for several courses, armed with good intentions, only to fall behind or lose interest. Hence, it's vital to start with a clear objective. Are you learning to enhance your current role or aiming for a new one? Do you want to branch into a new industry or simply develop a hobby? Clarifying these goals will help in selecting courses that are aligned with your career aspirations and personal interests.

An essential tip for making the most out of online learning is not to shy away from paying for quality content. While there are numerous free resources, sometimes investing in a course can provide you better quality, up-to-date content, and official certification that can add significant value to your resume. Many platforms offer financial aid, so exploring these options can also make premium courses accessible.

But online learning isn't just about new qualifications. It's a way to remain culturally informed and dynamically active in a rapidly changing global marketplace. With continuous skill development, remote workers can pivot quickly, leveraging new knowledge to adapt to market changes. This adaptability is a critical asset in times when industries morph overnight due to technological advances.

Interestingly, some of the most valuable lessons online can't be translated into certificates. Consider enrolling in webinars or following podcasts that discuss soft skills like communication, empathy, and leadership. They teach you how to navigate the subtle nuances of virtual collaboration and help you stand out in a digital landscape where such skills are more valuable than ever.

Moreover, actively engaging in online forums or professional social networks like LinkedIn groups can further complement your learning. These platforms can offer real-time discourse on industry trends, shared experiences, and practical advice. Participating in such discussions can solidify your learning and bring theoretical knowledge into practical contexts.

Being accountable is another crucial factor for success in online learning. Setting aside dedicated study time each week, structuring your learning schedule into your daily routine, and perhaps even finding a learning buddy can help keep momentum. This partnership or study group not only provides motivation but also delivers different perspectives that can deepen your understanding and perspective.

Remember, online learning is not just a means to an end. It should be viewed as an ongoing journey of personal and professional evolution. By fostering a habit of continual learning, remote workers and freelancers can build a portfolio of skills, making them better equipped to meet and even shape the challenges of the future work environment.

Ultimately, as remote work reshuffles the deck of what constitutes a thriving career, those who embrace and harness the myriad opportunities for online learning will be best poised to adapt, survive, and succeed in a world that's perpetually on the move.

## Balancing Skill Development with Work

Finding time for skill development while managing a demanding workload can feel like walking a tightrope. Yet, it's a crucial balance to strike in a world that prizes both flexibility and adaptability. In remote work, where the boundaries between personal and professional life can blur quickly, prioritizing skill enhancement without letting work slip through the cracks requires a strategic approach. It's about carving out that space to grow while keeping up with your day-to-day responsibilities—a challenge indeed, but one filled with opportunities if handled wisely.

Remote work environments offer a unique advantage: the flexibility to learn on your own terms. Unlike traditional office settings, remote work allows you to structure your day around focused learning periods, whether it's a quick online course during lunch or a deep dive into a new software after hours. However, the same flexibility can also lead to distractions; thus, the key is to harness this autonomy effectively. Successful remote workers plan their days strategically, striking a delicate balance that incorporates regular skill development without compromising their current job responsibilities.

To begin with, it's essential to conduct a self-assessment of your current skills set. Understand where you stand in your career trajectory and identify areas needing improvement. This often entails asking questions like, "What skills will future roles require?" or "Which skills could increase my value in my current role?" With these answers, you can then pinpoint specific learning goals that align with your professional development objectives. Goal-setting is not merely an academic exercise; it aligns aspirations with concrete outcomes, inspiring focused pursuit.

Once objectives are set, time management becomes your next best tool. Implement time-blocking techniques, dedicating specific windows in your calendar solely for learning. Consistency proves vital here: even short, regular sessions can build substantial knowledge over time. Consider scheduling recurring calendar alerts to remind yourself to dive into learning mode, much like you would for an important work meeting. By treating learning as an essential task, you're less likely to deprioritize it amidst work demands.

A helpful technique is to weave learning into your daily tasks. If you're embarking on a project that requires using new software, take advantage of online tutorials or community forums. This approach not only helps integrate skill development into your routine tasks but also enables immediate application of acquired knowledge, reinforcing learning through practice. Moreover, leveraging your job as a learning platform fosters a conducive environment where growth and productivity coexist.

Collaboration with your manager or team leader can also facilitate skill development. Communicating your learning goals opens doors to new opportunities such as project involvement, mentorship, or even funding for courses. Managers can also provide invaluable feedback, guiding you towards resources or strategies for growth that you might not have considered. Investing in a dialogue about personal development with those who understand your work context can provide tailored insights to propel your learning journey.

Additionally, consider seeking out communities that are focused on learning and development. Online forums, webinars, and professional groups—these spaces not only offer a wealth of knowledge but also opportunities to network with other professionals on a similar path. Engaging with a community can amplify motivation, keeping you inspired and informed about the latest industry trends and skills needed to remain competitive.

Meanwhile, it's important to remain adaptable. The skills landscape is ever-changing, with new tools and methodologies emerging rapidly. It requires a mindset open to continual change and re-learning. Rather than focusing solely on one area of expertise, broader skill sets enhance adaptability, making it easier to shift gears as industry demands evolve. Think of skills not as checkpoints to achieve, but as journeys of ongoing refinement and enhancement.

Outside structured learning, don't underestimate the power of informal education. Reading industry-related articles, watching webinars, or even listening to knowledgeable podcasts can contribute significantly to your development. These resources align with the modern remote worker's lifestyle, allowing learning to occur organically amid other tasks. They can be consumed in downtime or during activities like commuting or exercising, ensuring learning is ever-present, yet not overwhelming.

But balance is not just about adding more tasks; it also involves selective pruning. It's equally important to recognize and let go of activities that don't contribute meaningfully to your growth or productivity. This involves critically evaluating your workload to identify tasks that can be delegated or streamlined, freeing up bandwidth for skill development. It's about smartly allocating your limited resource—time—in a way that maximizes both present productivity and future potential.

For remote workers, maintaining work-life balance while focusing on self-improvement can require creative approaches, like setting physical cues to switch between work and learning modes. Whether it's a specific workspace change or a mental transition routine, separating these pursuits can enhance focus and experience. Ultimately, it's about finding what works for your personal rhythm and sticking with it.

In conclusion, expertly managing skill development alongside work tasks is less of a balancing act and more of a finely tuned orchestration. It demands self-awareness, strategic planning, and continued flexibility. But it also rewards with not only the mastery of new skills but also enriched work experiences and expanded career opportunities. As you grow, so will your ability to meet the demands of an ever-evolving remote work landscape—leading you to thrive professionally while enriching your personal development journey.

# Chapter 15: Remote Work in Different Cultures

In the vast and varied landscape of remote work, cultural nuances play a surprisingly significant role. As more companies tap into global talent pools and individuals choose flexible work lives, understanding these cultural differences becomes not just beneficial but essential. Remote work allows us to cross borders seamlessly, yet navigating these cultural waters demands empathy and adaptability.

One of the first hurdles is communication style. While some cultures value direct feedback and straightforward discourse, others may lean towards a more indirect or nuanced approach. It's important for remote workers to recognize and respect these differences, tailoring their communication to the context. Imagine working on a project with team members from both Japan and the United States. Your American colleagues might prefer getting straight to the point, while your Japanese team might find value in a more circular, consensus-driven discussion. Embracing this diversity can lead to more harmonious and productive collaboration.

Language barriers inevitably surface in such multicultural setups. However, they shouldn't be viewed as obstacles but rather as opportunities for growth. Learning a few phrases in your colleagues' native languages or investing in language learning tools shows respect and a willingness to bridge gaps. Even when misunderstandings occur, a sense of humor and patience can transform these moments into shared learning experiences.

Beyond communication, time perceptions can differ widely between cultures, influencing work expectations and deadlines. Some cultures perceive time as linear and rigid, while others take a more fluid, flexible approach. Understanding this can help mitigate frustrations and prevent miscommunications when coordinating projects. By cultivating an awareness and appreciation of these cultural differences, remote workers and managers can unlock the full potential of their diverse teams.

Adapting to cultural differences in remote work is not just about avoiding missteps. It's about enriching your own perspective and enhancing team cohesion. As we embrace this journey, we find that what's foreign today can become familiar tomorrow, leading to richer, more fulfilling work experiences for everyone involved.

## Adapting to Cultural Differences

Remote work transcends borders, allowing us to collaborate with people from diverse cultural backgrounds. This cultural tapestry can enrich our work and expand our perspectives, but it can also present unique challenges. Understanding and adapting to cultural differences becomes vital in fostering effective communication, collaboration, and mutual respect in a virtual workspace.

Every culture has its unwritten rules and nuances. The way people approach work can vary tremendously depending on their cultural background. Some cultures emphasize hierarchy and formal communication, while others prefer egalitarian and informal interactions. Being aware of these differences can prevent misunderstandings and foster smoother collaborations. It's crucial to keep an open mind and be willing to learn from others.

Consider the way time is perceived in different cultures. In some, punctuality is a sign of respect, while others may have a more relaxed approach. Misalignments in expectations about time can lead to frustration. Thus, it's important to establish clear communication about deadlines and meeting times. You might even find it helpful to adopt flexible working hours to accommodate team members in different time zones.

Language, although it is covered more deeply in the next section, is another aspect where cultural differences play a vital role. While English has become the lingua franca in many international remote work settings, language barriers still exist. Even among fluent English speakers, differing dialects and colloquialisms can create confusion. It's wise to use clear and simple language and, whenever possible, confirm understanding through feedback.

Beyond language, consider communication styles. Some cultures value directness, seeing it as a path to clear and efficient communication, while others may view it as rude. The latter might prefer a more indirect style, using context rather than explicit statements to convey their message. Adapting to these varied styles might involve toning down assertiveness or learning to read between the lines, depending on your audience.

Mannerisms and body language also vary. In video meetings, be mindful of gestures and facial expressions. What is a friendly nod in one culture could be interpreted differently in another. When in doubt, it's useful to explicitly ask for clarification. This not only avoids misinterpretation but also shows your willingness to understand and respect cultural differences.

Ways of expressing emotions and handling conflict also differ. In some cultures, open expression of feelings is common and accepted, while others may view it as unprofessional. Understanding these differences can aid in conflict resolution and help maintain harmonious working relationships. Encouraging a culture of empathy and patience can facilitate smoother interactions when emotions run high.

Holidays and working periods can also differ significantly. What's a standard workday in one part of the world may be a national holiday elsewhere. Respecting these cultural distinctions shows consideration and can improve team morale. Planning ahead and using shared holiday calendars can help accommodate everybody's schedules and ensure smooth project timelines.

Embracing cultural diversity in remote work settings can lead to greater innovation. Different perspectives foster creativity and offer unique solutions to problems. By leveraging the strengths each culture brings, teams can build inclusive products and solutions that are globally appealing and accessible.

Building cultural intelligence takes effort and intention. It involves being observant, asking questions, and being willing to adapt. Simple actions like researching cultural norms or reaching out to colleagues with questions can demonstrate a commitment to understanding and respect. Many organizations now offer cultural competency training, which can be invaluable for teams working across borders.

Perhaps most importantly, adaptivity to cultural differences can deepen the connections we form in remote teams. It can transform a simple work project into a valuable learning experience. This fosters an inclusive work environment where every voice feels heard and valued, ultimately contributing to the success of the team.

Adapting to cultural differences is not just about avoiding misunderstandings; it's about embracing and celebrating the diversity that remote work naturally brings. In doing so, remote workers and managers alike will find themselves not only thriving in this new paradigm but also growing personally and professionally.

## Overcoming Language Barriers

The rise of remote work has opened doors to global talent, allowing teams from diverse linguistic backgrounds to collaborate seamlessly. Yet, language differences can pose significant challenges, potentially disrupting communication and teamwork. It's essential to address these barriers head-on to ensure smooth and effective collaboration in today's multicultural work environments. With the right strategies, language diversity can evolve from a challenge into an invaluable asset, enhancing creativity and problem-solving through a rich tapestry of perspectives.

The foundation of overcoming language barriers begins with fostering an inclusive culture that values communication. Encouraging team members to express themselves freely, even if their language skills aren't perfect, sets the tone for openness and adaptation. Pairing this with a genuine willingness to understand and learn from each other's linguistic differences can create a supportive environment where everyone feels valued and heard. Encouragement goes a long way, and when individuals feel comfortable making mistakes, they are more likely to contribute and collaborate effectively.

Technology plays a pivotal role in bridging language divides. Tools like real-time translation services and language learning apps can help break down communication barriers instantly. These digital aids can reduce misunderstandings and facilitate more precise exchanges, making them indispensable in a remote setting. However, it's crucial to recognize that technology, while helpful, isn't a standalone solution. The human element of patience, empathy, and cultural sensitivity must accompany technological interventions to achieve the best results.

Investing time in learning key phrases or basic language skills of your international colleagues shows respect and can profoundly impact team dynamics. This doesn't mean achieving fluency in multiple languages but rather acquiring enough understanding to appreciate nuances and build rapport. A small effort in learning a colleague's language can demonstrate commitment to the team and enhance mutual respect, potentially opening up lines of communication that were previously blocked.

Language isn't just about words; it's a gateway to understanding cultural contexts and references. Thus, developing cultural awareness alongside language skills is essential. This might involve exploring cultural traditions, business etiquettes, or communication styles prevalent in colleagues' countries. By doing so, team members can avoid potential misinterpretations and foster an atmosphere of mutual respect and understanding. Cultural competence forms the backbone of effective multilingual communication.

Regular cross-cultural training sessions and workshops can also be significant in addressing language obstacles. These sessions provide opportunities to explore common challenges and develop strategies collectively. Role-playing scenarios, team building exercises, or storytelling sessions can make such training engaging and insightful. Teams can also explore different cultural communication styles, enhancing empathy and patience when dialogue occasionally falters. In turn, this nurtures a spirit of collaboration and a willingness to learn from one another.

Additionally, establishing a common working language can streamline communication processes significantly in diverse teams. English often serves this role in international business contexts, but its use should be flexible, accommodating everybody's proficiency levels. Providing language assistance, such as translating key documents or offering language support for team meetings, can help avoid alienating non-native speakers. It's important for team leaders to reinforce the idea that it's the shared goal, rather than perfect language proficiency, that truly matters.

Leveraging asynchronous communication can also mitigate language barriers by giving team members the time they need to compose thoughtful responses or translations of messages. This can reduce the pressure associated with immediate verbal exchanges, allowing individuals to contribute more meaningfully. Asynchronous tools like email, chat platforms, and collaborative documents can enable team members to process information at their own pace, ensuring accuracy and confidence in their contributions.

Feedback loops play an essential role in refining communicative strategies further. By establishing a culture of feedback, teams can identify language-related bottlenecks and successes, adapting their methods to improve over time. Constructive feedback helps individuals learn from each other and adjust, fostering an environment where language barriers become less daunting and more surmountable. Consistent feedback nurtures a learning environment where improvements are celebrated and mistakes are viewed as learning opportunities.

Finally, remember that overcoming language barriers in a remote work setting is an ongoing journey rather than a one-time box to check. As teams evolve, new members bring different languages and cultural dynamics, continually reshaping communication requirements. By maintaining an adaptive approach, fostering openness, and dedicating time to understanding both linguistic and cultural diversity, teams can harness these differences and transform them into strengths that drive innovation and growth.

Embracing language diversity not only enriches team collaboration but also broadens perspectives, fostering creativity and innovation. As remote work continues to forge connections across borders, understanding and overcoming language barriers will be key to building resilient, harmonious, and dynamic teams. The aim isn't solely fluent communication, but a shared sense of purpose and commitment to mutual understanding that transcends words. Let language differences not divide, but unite us towards achieving common goals with enriched perspectives and newfound strength.

# Chapter 16: Security and Privacy

In the intricate dance of remote work, security and privacy take center stage as critical elements that ensure the tranquility of our virtual office spaces. As a remote worker, whether you're a freelance entrepreneur or an agile manager, the sanctity of your digital environment is paramount. A breach not only threatens your data but can also disrupt workflows and erode client trust. In a world where connectivity fuels productivity, understanding how to safeguard your digital realm is non-negotiable.

At the heart of security and privacy concerns lies the personal data stored on your devices and the cloud. This data, ranging from your email credentials to sensitive business documents, must be zealously protected against cyber threats. Begin by adopting a mindset where security is integral to your daily operations. It's essential to cultivate habits like using strong, unique passwords for every account and enabling two-factor authentication wherever possible. Simple as they may seem, these steps can act as your first line of defense against unauthorized access.

Encryption is another powerhouse tool in securing your remote workspace. Think of encryption as converting your sensitive data into a complex code that only authorized users can decipher. Utilizing tools and services that offer end-to-end encryption means ensuring your messages and files are unintelligible to prying eyes. This is especially vital when working with sensitive client information or proprietary company data over the internet. Whether it's email communications or cloud storage, prioritize solutions that offer robust encryption options.

Understanding the basics of cybersecurity doesn't require an in-depth technical background, but it does demand a proactive approach. Awareness is your greatest ally. Stay informed about common phishing and social engineering tactics, as cybercriminals often exploit human psychology more than technical vulnerabilities. If a request seems off—even if it comes from a known contact—pause, verify, and trust your instincts. These scams can range from cleverly disguised emails that urge password resets to phone calls pretending to be from tech support.

Remote work environments often mean connecting from multiple locations, yet each network connection represents a potential vulnerability. Public Wi-Fi networks are notoriously insecure; connecting to a coffee shop network without precautions can expose your data to interception. A Virtual Private Network (VPN) is an essential tool to secure your internet connection, making it virtually impenetrable while masking your IP address. Consider it an obligatory component of your security toolkit whenever you step outside your home network.

While technology underpins the remote work landscape, never underestimate the human element of security. Regularly updating software and applications ensures you benefit from the latest security patches. Encourage a culture of security within your team or yourself by routinely discussing and reviewing your privacy settings and security features. After all, fostering a secure mindset is a collective responsibility in any thriving remote work ecosystem.

Embracing security and privacy as foundational elements of remote work liberates you to focus on creativity and productivity without the looming shadow of data breaches. Equip yourself with these strategies and tools not only to protect what matters most but also to inspire confidence in your collaborative ventures. As we navigate through the complexities of the digital world, let security and privacy be the stable compass guiding our safe and efficient journey.

## Protecting Your Data

In our rapidly evolving remote work landscape, the importance of data protection looms larger than ever. You're not just working with files and figures; you're handling sensitive information that deserves vigilant protection. Regardless of whether you're a seasoned freelancer or managing a remote team, understanding the fundamentals of data security can safeguard not only your work but your reputation as well.

Let's start with recognizing the value of your data. Confidential information, client contracts, and proprietary research—all this data isn't just valuable to you but could be equally enticing to malicious entities. It's essential to treat your digital assets with the same care you'd give to your physical ones. Consider data protection as an ongoing responsibility, not merely a checklist to complete.

First and foremost, strong passwords are your frontline defense. While this might sound straightforward, too many people underestimate their worth. Think of your passwords as keys to a vault. They should be complex, perhaps a mix of uppercase and lowercase letters, numbers, and symbols. Also, avoid using the same password across multiple platforms to minimize risk. A reliable password manager can assist in creating and storing secure passwords, making it easier to maintain unique access credentials across various services.

Two-factor authentication (2FA) offers an additional layer of security. It ensures that even if your password is compromised, unauthorized access remains distant. Implementing 2FA is simple and effective. It often uses something you know (your password) and something you have (a text message or mobile app confirmation) to grant access to your data. Many service providers support 2FA, and it's wise to enable this feature wherever available.

Storing and sharing data safely is another critical aspect. Cloud services provide robust solutions for remote collaboration, but understanding their security measures is key. Ensure that your provider employs encryption not only when data is at rest but also while in transit. Encryption translates your data into complex code, necessary for preventing unauthorized access.

When choosing a cloud storage service, read their privacy policy carefully. Familiarize yourself with how they handle and protect your data. If your work involves handling highly sensitive information, you might even consider services that offer end-to-end encryption, which adds another layer of protection.

Regular software updates shouldn't be overlooked. Updates aren't just about adding new features; they often patch security vulnerabilities. Make it a habit to update your software, plugins, and operating systems promptly. Automatic updates or reminders can significantly ease this process, ensuring your defensive wall remains uncompromised.

Virtual Private Networks (VPNs) are fantastic tools for maintaining a secure online presence, especially when accessing public Wi-Fi. VPNs reroute your internet connection through secure servers, masking your IP address and encrypting your data. This helps protect against cyber threats when working from cafes or public libraries, locations where network security isn't guaranteed.

Predominantly, avoiding phishing attempts is pivotal. Phishing remains one of the most common cyber threats, where attackers disguise themselves as trustworthy entities through emails or messages to extract personal information. Be skeptical of unsolicited communications and avoid clicking on suspicious links or attachments. Remember, a healthy dose of skepticism is a valuable trait in data protection.

Another layer of defense: backups. Regularly backing up your data ensures that you have another copy of important information in case of accidental loss or cyber-attacks. Utilize both cloud-based solutions and physical external drives for storing backups, keeping them updated frequently.

For those managing a team, fostering a culture of security awareness is crucial. Conduct regular training sessions to keep everyone informed of the latest threats and best practices. Establish clear security protocols and ensure all team members understand and follow them. This collective vigilance promotes a secure environment, where everyone plays a part in safeguarding the organization's data.

Lastly, be mindful of your digital footprint. Understand what personal information you share online and how it could potentially be used against you. Regularly audit your social media privacy settings to keep your personal and professional lives appropriately divided.

In conclusion, protecting your data in a remote work setting involves a combination of tools, practices, and mindset shifts. While the task may feel daunting, approaching it step-by-step makes it manageable. Remember, security is not a one-time effort but a continuous journey.

Your proactive measures in data protection not only fortify your work but also build trust with clients and colleagues, affirming your commitment to security and excellence in a decentralized world.

## Understanding Cybersecurity Basics

In an era where remote work is rapidly becoming the norm, understanding the foundations of cybersecurity isn't just a bonus—it's a necessity. The acceleration of remote work can supercharge productivity and provide unparalleled flexibility. However, it also exposes individuals to an array of cyber risks. This section will delve into the fundamental concepts of cybersecurity that remote workers, freelancers, and managers need to be aware of, ensuring that your digital workspace remains secure.

Let's start with the basics: what exactly is cybersecurity? In essence, cybersecurity is the practice of protecting systems, networks, and programs from digital attacks. These cyberattacks aim to access, change, or destroy sensitive information; extort money from users; or interrupt normal business processes. For remote workers, understanding these threats means recognizing the need for safeguarding not just devices, but also the data and networks in use. It's about creating a secure environment that minimizes risk while maximizing connectivity.

Consider the various digital devices you employ for work from laptops to smartphones and tablets. Each of these devices can be a potential gateway for cyber threats. Simple measures, like using strong, unique passwords and enabling two-factor authentication, can go a long way in defending against unauthorized access. In today's work-from-anywhere culture, maintaining these practices becomes second nature. Think of them as the digital equivalent of locking the front door when leaving home.

The human factor also plays a significant role in cybersecurity. Often, cybercriminals exploit people rather than technology. Phishing attacks, for instance, are designed to trick individuals into disclosing sensitive information, such as passwords or financial information. Remote workers should be vigilant against suspicious emails or messages and verify the authenticity of communication before responding. Understanding the psychology behind these attacks offers empowerment and helps build a more formidable defense.

One cannot overlook the importance of securing the networks we rely on every day. Public Wi-Fi networks, although convenient, pose significant security risks. These networks are often unencrypted, making it easier for attackers to intercept data. Utilizing a virtual private network (VPN) encrypts your connection and provides an additional layer of protection, making it a crucial tool for anyone working remotely from coffee shops, co-working spaces, or even home.

Let's not forget the data itself—one of the most prized assets in our digital lives. Data encryption transforms your valuable information into a secure format that can only be accessed by those with the correct decryption key. Employing encryption for both stored data and data in transit is essential. Whether it's sensitive client information or personal financial details, encrypting this data shields you from devastating losses.

The way we store data also matters. Cloud services have transformed how we store, share, and manage information, offering benefits like accessibility and reduced reliance on physical storage. Yet, the cloud introduces its own set of cyber risks. Remote workers must ensure they choose reputable cloud providers with robust security measures. Always be sure to regularly update software and applications to patch vulnerabilities, keeping cyber threats at bay.

Beyond the tools and techniques, cultivating a culture of awareness and continuous learning significantly bolsters security. Cyber threats evolve, and so should our understanding and responses to them. Engaging in regular cybersecurity training and staying informed about the latest threats and best practices is invaluable. It's not just about protecting what you have today, but also about staying ahead of what's coming tomorrow.

Cybersecurity is indeed a shared responsibility. As remote workers, it involves collaboration not only with IT professionals but also with colleagues and clients to ensure a unified defense approach. Communication about security policies, potential threats, and best practices should be clear, consistent, and participatory. By encouraging an open dialogue about cybersecurity, individuals contribute to a safer and more trusted remote working environment.

In conclusion, understanding cybersecurity basics is less about fearing what might happen and more about taking proactive steps toward peaceful productivity. By equipping yourself with the right knowledge and tools, you won't just guard against threats—you'll empower your professional journey, embracing the freedom and flexibility remote work offers without compromise. Security and privacy are not just features of technology; they are foundational to sustainable success in today's decentralized work environment.

# Chapter 17: The Future of Remote Work

Remote work wasn't a fleeting trend; it's here to stay. As we look to the future, it's crucial to adapt to the rapidly changing landscape while maintaining balance and innovation. With companies embracing more flexible work arrangements, the potential for technological advancement is vast. We must stay at the forefront to harness these changes effectively. Embracing innovation isn't just about adopting new tools; it's about nurturing a mindset ready to adapt and evolve continually.

Collaboration will mean something entirely different in the years to come. Imagine a workspace where virtual reality bridges geographical gaps, offering a sense of presence that transcends screens. As automation assumes repetitive tasks, humans will focus more on creative and strategic roles. This shift will redefine job descriptions and workplace dynamics, demanding new skills and adaptability. It's important to actively seek out learning opportunities to future-proof our careers in this evolving landscape.

Furthermore, the future will likely see a more profound integration of AI in everyday workflows. This raises challenges and opportunities alike. The challenge lies in ensuring these technologies align with human values, enhancing productivity without sacrificing the human touch. Opportunities present themselves in how these advancements can improve work-life balance, potentially reshaping how "work" itself is defined.

Understanding and anticipating these changes is crucial, not just for staying relevant but for thriving in your career. Start building a robust professional network now. Engaging with these communities will provide insight, support, and inspiration as we navigate this complex future together. The exciting journey of remote work is unpredictable, yet filled with endless possibilities. Let's embrace this future with open minds and resilience.

## Predicting Industry Changes

As remote work continues to redefine traditional office boundaries, predicting the changes in various industries can guide how we adapt and thrive in this evolving landscape. Understanding the trajectory of industry shifts involves recognizing trends, anticipating challenges, and embracing innovation. As we delve into predicting industry changes, it's crucial to approach this topic with both a strategic mindset and an open heart, recognizing the broader impacts on our personal and professional lives.

One of the most profound shifts we anticipate is the transformation in how companies recognize and nurture talent. Traditional metrics like time spent in the office are giving way to results-oriented performance evaluation. This change emphasizes the importance of accountability and skill over mere presence, presenting remote workers with the opportunity to showcase their true value. Such a shift allows individuals to take control of their careers, nurturing a personal brand defined by outcomes and creativity rather than how visible they are at a desk.

Industries will also witness a significant transformation in their hiring practices. Remote work breaks geographical barriers, opening up talent pools across the globe. Companies are no longer limited by local hiring constraints, enabling a richer diversity of ideas and perspectives. However, this global competition also means individuals may need to develop niche skills or unique expertise to stand out. By remaining committed to continuous learning and skill enhancement, remote workers can position themselves at the forefront of their industries, ready to seize emerging opportunities.

The real estate and infrastructure sectors face equally fascinating changes. As remote work proves its staying power, companies are rethinking their office space needs. We may see a reduction in traditional office spaces, replaced by versatile hubs designed for occasional in-person collaborations. This shift presents an opportunity for cities and real estate developers to rethink urban planning, integrating flexible work hubs that blend seamlessly into communal spaces. Moreover, rural areas could experience a renaissance as workers take advantage of no longer being tethered to urban centers, seeking lifestyles that promise better work-life balance.

Education systems must also adapt. With schools having delivered education remotely during the pandemic, we're likely to see curricula evolve to incorporate digital learning tools permanently. This change mandates a curriculum that not only focuses on knowledge acquisition but also emphasizes skills essential for remote work: communication, digital literacy, and self-discipline. Educational institutions need to prepare students with skills relevant to a future where adaptability is paramount.

Technology will continue to be a critical driver of these changes. The rise of virtual and augmented reality may redefine not just workspaces but the very nature of interpersonal interactions. Imagine virtual meeting rooms that replicate in-person interactions more closely or training sessions conducted through immersive experiences. Harnessing such technology can strengthen team bonds and improve collaborative efforts, regardless of physical location.

While automation and artificial intelligence continue to emerge as transformative forces, they may redefine job roles across various sectors rather than eliminate them. Instead of fearing automation as a replacement, consider it a catalyst for redefining and enhancing human skill sets. Remote workers can leverage automation to eliminate mundane tasks, focusing instead on creative and strategic work that truly adds value. Industries must embrace a vision where humans and machines collaborate seamlessly to drive unprecedented growth and innovation.

Of course, with change comes challenge. Organizations will need to address cybersecurity concerns more seriously than ever, as decentralized work increases vulnerability to potential threats. Developing robust security protocols and fostering a culture of vigilance will be pivotal to safeguarding data integrity. Remote workers must also stay informed about best practices in security, ensuring that they become part of the solution rather than a liability. Trust will become a cornerstone of the remote work ethos, guiding interactions and decisions.

The way companies structure benefits and compensation will likely undergo a significant transformation. As organizations save on costs associated with physical office spaces, they might redirect these savings to support employees' holistic needs, such as wellness programs tailored for remote lifestyles, technology stipends, or flexible schedules. This emerging paradigm emphasizes well-being and personal development as integral components of employment, rather than mere perks.

Industries that have traditionally resisted remote work, such as finance or law, may find themselves gradually embracing the shift as technology renders virtual collaboration more seamless and secure. The challenge for these sectors is to balance regulatory compliance with technological advancements, ensuring that remote operations maintain the same standards of excellence and confidentiality as their traditional counterparts. Leaders in these fields must envision new frameworks that support remote engagements without compromising their core principles.

As businesses further integrate remote work into their culture, there's a potential for reshaping company values and objectives. Leadership will pivot towards inclusivity, empathy, and sustained engagement, recognizing that a distributed workforce thrives on shared purpose and genuine connection. Organizations that embrace and embody such values will foster greater loyalty, creativity, and resilience among their teams, ensuring sustained success in a world that values adaptability above all else.

In this shifting landscape, the role of leadership is more critical than ever. Leaders must not only be adept at navigating the technological demands of remote work but must also empathetically manage the human aspects of this transition. Building a culture that thrives on trust, inclusivity, and open communication can empower teams to reach new heights. As leadership evolves, so too must their strategies for fostering collaboration and innovation within dispersed teams.

Ultimately, predicting industry changes in the realm of remote work hinges on our ability to envision a future that embraces flexibility, diversity, and innovation. By strategically aligning with these emerging trends, remote workers, freelancers, and managers can transform challenges into opportunities. As we navigate these shifts together, the path forward becomes not just about adapting but about advancing with intention and purpose. Here's to shaping a future of work that's not just different, but markedly better for every one of us involved.

## The Role of Automation

As the landscape of remote work continues to evolve, automation is emerging as a crucial element, reshaping how we approach tasks, manage time, and drive productivity. Automation isn't just about replacing manual processes; it's about enhancing our capabilities, freeing up time for more innovative and creative endeavors. For remote workers and managers alike, understanding and leveraging automation can be a powerful asset.

At its core, automation is about efficiency and consistency. It helps eliminate repetitive tasks, ensuring that time and energy are directed towards more meaningful work. Imagine starting your day with a clean slate—emails sorted, reports generated, routine tasks handled. It's not just a dream; many remote workers are already living it, thanks to a multitude of automation tools available today.

Think about the potential impact on productivity. With fewer mundane tasks to worry about, remote workers can focus on complex problem-solving, strategizing, and creativity. For managers, automation in workflows and communication allows a more streamlined approach, maintaining oversight without micromanagement. It's about trusting the process to handle the groundwork so that human skills can shine in areas that matter most.

Automation can also enhance communication in remote work environments. Tools that auto-schedule meetings, follow up on tasks, or send reminders help ensure that remote teams stay in sync across time zones. These systems mitigate the risk of human oversight, ensuring a seamless flow of information and collaboration. It doesn't just make life easier; it enables teams to become more cohesive and connected, even if they're physically apart.

However, embracing automation in remote work isn't without its challenges. It requires a shift in mindset and a willingness to adapt to new technologies. Some may fear the loss of control or the dehumanization of work, but it's crucial to remember that automation is a tool, not a replacement for human ingenuity. It's there to complement and enhance our skills, not to overshadow them.

Ensuring smooth integration of automation into a remote work setup involves choosing the right tools that align with your work style and goals. It's about customizing your toolkit to not only include robust project management software but also tools that capture the nuances of your everyday tasks. This might mean integrating software that handles everything from generating invoices to optimizing content marketing strategies.

Consider the necessity of continuous learning. The tools and systems we use today may not be the same tomorrow. Embracing automation also means staying ahead of the curve, always ready to learn, and adapt. Online courses, webinars, and community forums are excellent resources for remote workers to keep enhancing their skill sets, ensuring they remain competent and competitive as automation technology advances.

The role of automation goes beyond individual productivity—it also impacts how organizations structure their teams. By embracing automation, companies can explore new models for collaboration and communication, such as flatter hierarchies and more dynamic teams. This shift can lead to greater innovation and faster decision-making, crucial assets in a rapidly changing market.

For freelancers and entrepreneurs, automation opens up novel avenues for scaling their efforts. By automating administrative tasks, they can focus on expanding their businesses or pursuing new projects. It's about creating a sustainable work-life balance where the technology works for you, not against you. The time saved can be redirected towards client relationships, strategic planning, or even personal development.

Yet, with all its benefits, automation should not be seen as a panacea for all remote work challenges. It's crucial to maintain a balance, ensuring that technology supports and doesn't overwhelm. This involves regularly evaluating the tools and processes in place—are they boosting productivity or becoming an additional layer of complexity? Being intentional about this balance helps keep the work environment both efficient and human-centric.

In conclusion, the role of automation in the future of remote work is monumental and multifaceted. It's a powerful enabler that, when harnessed effectively, can transform how we work and interact. The future lies in a hybrid approach where human intuition and technology come together, enhancing our capabilities and opening new frontiers in remote work. As remote workers, freelancers, and managers, embracing this change with an open mind can lead to greater productivity, innovation, and fulfillment.

# Chapter 18: Health and Well-Being

Remote work offers unparalleled flexibility and freedom. However, ensuring our health and well-being needs remain equally important. It's easy to slip into patterns that neglect physical and mental health when your home doubles as your office. Deliberate strategies and conscious choices can keep our well-being front and center.

Physical health forms the cornerstone of overall well-being. Regular movement is crucial, especially when your commute is just a short walk to your desk. It might seem small, but scheduling brief exercise sessions or simply stretching throughout the day can significantly impact your energy levels. Whether it's a morning jog or a quick yoga session, these activities restore vitality and keep stress at bay.

Equally important is mental health. Practices such as mindfulness or meditation can enhance focus and reduce anxiety. It's about creating spaces in your day to step back and breathe. Technology, while a boon, can overwhelm. Thus, setting boundaries with devices and social media helps in tuning out the noise, allowing tranquil moments to thrive.

A healthy work-life balance supports both physical and mental health. Allow yourself downtime post-work hours to pursue hobbies or connect with loved ones. This separation fosters not only relaxation but enriches professional productivity. Every boundary needs to be firm yet flexible to adapt to varying demands, while ensuring you don't burn out.

Finally, consider the environment. A home office that feels comfortable yet inspiring can make all the difference. Incorporating plants, adequate lighting, and perhaps calming colors can create a setting that's conducive to both work and well-being. This holistic approach integrates your work environment into your wellness strategy, promoting harmony and efficiency.

Recognizing the intricate relationship between productivity and health is the first step towards thriving in a remote setting. Take initiative in crafting a lifestyle where professional success doesn't come at the expense of personal well-being. Set the stage for sustained health, both in body and spirit.

## Maintaining Physical Health

While remote work offers countless benefits, it also presents unique challenges to maintaining physical health. You're not compelled to leave your home, and without a traditional office routine, the lines between work, rest, and exercise can blur. In this environment, prioritizing physical health isn't just essential; it's transformative. Staying physically active boosts your energy, enhances productivity, and even improves your mental health.

A significant aspect of maintaining physical health in a remote work setting is understanding the importance of movement and breaking up long periods of sitting. It's easy to find yourself glued to your desk for hours without realizing how much time has passed. Introducing structured breaks and incorporating physical activity into your daily routine can make a world of difference. Whether it's a five-minute stretch every hour or a brisk walk around the block during lunch, these moments of movement are vital for combating the sedentary lifestyle that remote work can encourage.

Establishing a regular exercise routine is one of the most productive habits you can cultivate. Unlike commuting to a gym, working out from home offers flexibility and convenience, allowing you to tailor your exercise regimen to your personal preferences and schedule. Whether you enjoy yoga, cycling, or strength training, there's an abundance of online classes and apps that can guide and motivate you. The key is consistency. Aim for a realistic goal, such as 30 minutes a day, and adjust as you see fit.

Creating a dedicated space for exercise at home can also enhance your commitment to physical health. This doesn't mean transforming a room into a gym but finding a spot where you can comfortably move. A yoga mat and perhaps a few weights or resistance bands can quickly turn a corner of your home into a personal fitness hub. An inspiring and clutter-free environment is more inviting and can serve as a powerful motivation to keep up with your workouts.

Ergonomics play a crucial role in sustaining physical health while working remotely. An uncomfortable workstation not only affects your comfort but can also lead to long-term health issues. Investing in a chair with adequate support and a desk at the proper height is more than just a matter of comfort; it's a requirement for maintaining good posture and preventing strains. Adjust your monitor to eye level and ensure your wrists are straight when typing. These adjustments might seem small, but they bring considerable benefits over time.

The role of nutrition in maintaining physical health cannot be understated, especially when working from home. With easy access to the kitchen, it's tempting to graze throughout the day or resort to convenience foods. Planning balanced meals and healthy snacks helps maintain steady energy levels and supports overall well-being. Batch cooking on weekends can make it easier to avoid the temptation of unhealthy options when deadlines loom.

Hydration, often overlooked, is another critical element. A well-hydrated body functions optimally, aids in concentration, and supports sustained productivity. Keep a bottle of water at your desk and set reminders to drink regularly if necessary. Making a habit of reaching for water rather than caffeine or sugar-laden beverages can improve how you feel and function throughout the workday.

Stress management is inherently linked to physical health. While mental health strategies are covered later, it's vital to acknowledge the interplay between stress and physical well-being here. Integrating activities like meditation or deep breathing exercises into your daily routine can alleviate stress and its physical manifestations. Physical exercise, too, acts as a potent stress-reliever, helping reduce anxiety and improve mood.

Social interaction, albeit virtual, plays a part in your physical health. Regularly engaging with colleagues or joining virtual fitness groups can provide a sense of community and accountability. This social element can encourage you to remain active and remind you that you're not alone in prioritizing your physical health journey, no matter the distance.

It's equally essential to recognize the potential of seasonal and environmental influences on your physical health. Natural light exposure, for instance, profoundly impacts your sleep and mood. Arrange your workspace to maximize daylight and consider outdoor activities as a means to bolster your vitamin D intake and maintain a healthy circadian rhythm.

Lastly, listen to your body. The freedom of remote work allows you to be more attuned to your own needs. If you're feeling fatigued or in pain, acknowledge it and adjust your routine accordingly. Rest is as crucial as activity.

Working remotely affords a unique opportunity to integrate health practices into daily life with unprecedented flexibility. By adopting a proactive approach to physical health, you not only enhance your quality of life but also, ultimately, your work performance. Embrace these strategies not as obligatory chores, but as enriching habits that will benefit you personally and professionally.

## Mental Health Strategies

In the dynamic realm of remote work, maintaining mental health isn't just important; it's essential. While the potential for flexibility and autonomy is vast, the risks of isolation, burnout, and stress often loom large. Understanding and implementing strategies to protect and enhance mental well-being can transform the way you engage with your work and life.

One of the most potent tools for safeguarding mental health is establishing and maintaining a daily routine. This concept, though seemingly simple, becomes a beacon of stability in an otherwise fluid work environment. Consistent routines provide structure and predictability, helping to regulate stress and improve focus. Embrace routines that include a balance of work tasks, breaks, physical activity, and personal time to recharge. Incorporate regular start and end times for your workday, even if your hours are flexible. This separation makes a significant difference in letting your mind know when it's in 'work mode' and when it's time to wind down.

Another vital strategy is nurturing your physical health, which is intricately connected to your mental state. Regular exercise is often heralded for its physical benefits, but its impact on mental health is profoundly significant. Exercise releases endorphins, which can boost mood, decrease stress, and increase mental sharpness. It doesn't have to be daunting; even a brisk 30-minute walk or a quick home workout can work wonders. Schedule these activities just as you would a business meeting. They're non-negotiable 'appointments' with yourself.

Mindfulness and meditation have become mainstream recommendations for a reason. In the hustle and bustle of driving remote projects or juggling multiple clients, taking moments to breathe and clear your mind can reduce anxiety and improve concentration. Techniques like deep breathing, visualization, or guided meditation can be seamlessly integrated into your daily routine. Begin with just a few minutes each day, using mobile apps or online resources that guide you through the process. Gradually increase the time as you find your rhythm.

Cultivating a support network is another cornerstone of mental health. Remote work can often feel like drifting through a digital desert, where genuine human interaction feels sparse. However, maintaining personal and professional relationships can illuminate the way forward. Use video calls instead of emails or texts when it matters, partake in virtual coffee breaks with colleagues, and don't shy away from reaching out for help. Online communities for remote workers are also excellent spaces to share experiences and advice, creating a sense of belonging that persists despite physical distances.

Setting boundaries is paramount to prevent burnout. The blend of living and workspaces can erode the boundaries between professional responsibilities and personal life. It's crucial to delineate time and space for work, rest, and play. Notify your household of your work hours and keep your workplace distinct, even if it's a specific corner in a room. Technology can be both a friend and foe; use digital tools to mark your presence online but also leverage them to establish limits, such as using apps that restrict access to work email after hours.

Don't forget the power of lifelong learning for mental stimulation and fulfillment. Engaging in learning activities unrelated to your immediate work demands can be invigorating and broaden your horizons. Whether it's mastering a new language, delving into creative writing, or understanding a different aspect of technology, these pursuits nourish the mind and provide a healthy distraction from work-related stress.

It's equally important to recognize when professional help is needed. Remote environments might intensify feelings of isolation and anxiety, and there's no shame in seeking support. Virtual therapy options have made mental health support more accessible than ever. Platforms offering online counseling or therapy services can bridge the gap and provide professional assistance without the need for physical meetings. Prioritizing mental health means knowing when and how to ask for help.

In conclusion, developing mental health strategies is an ongoing process that's personalized for each individual. There's no one-size-fits-all solution, but with mindfulness, clear boundaries, and self-care, it's possible to thrive in remote work settings. By actively nurturing mental health, remote workers and freelancers can unlock their potential, enhancing productivity and cultivating happiness in both their personal and professional lives. The world of remote work is here to stay, and with these strategies, you are equipped not just to survive, but to flourish.

# Chapter 19: Creative Professions in a Remote Setting

In the ever-evolving landscape of remote work, creative professionals find themselves at an intriguing crossroads. It's a place where artistic spontaneity meets the structured realm of digital connectivity. The freedom to create across borders, while invigorating, also necessitates a reimagining of collaboration and inspiration. The challenge is to nurture creativity when the vibrant studio environment becomes a solitary room or a bustling café.

For artists, designers, writers, musicians, and other creatives, working remotely offers a unique opportunity to redefine their creative space. Gone are the barriers of geography that once dictated artistic collaborations. Now, a writer in New York can craft narratives alongside an illustrator in Tokyo, all in real-time and with an immediacy never before possible. Digital tools like graphic tablets, music production software, and collaborative platforms bridge these distances, enabling a fusion of diverse talents that can yield remarkable results.

The shift to remote settings also presents an invitation to explore creative resilience. Inspiration can bloom anywhere, and for many creatives, new surroundings offer fresh perspectives. Sometimes, a change in physical environment—even temporarily relocating from a traditional office space to a park bench or a sunny patio—can ignite a creative spark. It's about finding that sweet spot where comfort meets unpredictability, allowing imaginations to roam freely.

Yet, this autonomy isn't without its hurdles. Isolation can be a double-edged sword for the creative spirit, both a muse and a menace. While solitude often births deep focus, prolonged seclusion can stifle creativity and motivation. Building a virtual community or a network of like-minded creatives is vital. Platforms like Slack, Zoom, and collaborative apps provide arenas where ideas flow freely, critiques become learning moments, and encouragement is ever-present. These digital circles can mimic the camaraderie of physical studios, offering both connection and creative nourishment.

Moreover, establishing a routine that embraces flexibility can be transformative. Unlike the rigid 9-to-5, creative work often ebbs and flows, influenced by inspiration rather than the clock. Creative professionals in remote environments must learn to recognize and capitalize on their own rhythms. Some may find their peak creativity in the dead of night, others in the early morning light. The key is to create a structure that flexes to fit personal peaks while maintaining productivity.

Finally, the global nature of remote work opens doors to diverse perspectives, which can be a wellspring for innovation. Collaborations across cultures not only enhance creativity but also broaden the scope of what can be achieved. Different cultural influences and styles can be woven together to create unique, boundary-defying work that might otherwise not emerge within local confines.

The remote setting, then, isn't merely a backdrop for creativity; it's a canvas. By embracing new tools, seeking connection, and allowing flexibility to guide their work habits, creatives can thrive in this setting. The art of remote work lies in balancing solitude and community, spontaneity and structure, to create a masterpiece of one's own professional life.

## Opportunities for Artists and Creatives

In the fast-paced, ever-evolving realm of remote work, artists and creatives find themselves presented with unique opportunities that were unimaginable just a few decades ago. The digital age has reshaped how creative professionals express themselves, collaborate, and even earn a living. As remote work becomes more mainstream, artists can harness technology to not only showcase their talents but also to redefine traditional roles in creative industries.

Traditionally, artists and creatives often found themselves restricted to physical spaces and specific locales to reach their audience. Now, with the advent of remote platforms and tools, location-based barriers have been dismantled, allowing creatives to tap into global markets. Platforms like Instagram, Etsy, and even Patreon have transformed how artists connect with fans and patrons, providing them with avenues to display and sell their work on a global stage. This newfound accessibility is a powerful motivator, breathing life into creative visions that might have otherwise remained confined to local settings.

Moreover, remote work technologies have made it easier for creatives to collaborate without geographical limitations. Virtual tools such as collaborative design apps, cloud-based software, and video conferencing enable artists to engage with peers and clients from around the world. This expansion of creative networks not only enhances creative output but also spurs innovation through diverse collaborations that transcend cultural and geographical barriers.

Another significant opportunity lies in the realm of digital art and design. With the growing popularity of NFTs (Non-Fungible Tokens), artists have an entirely new digital marketplace ripe for exploration. This is a realm where creative talent truly shines, as it allows for innovation in how art is produced, sold, and owned. It challenges artists to think differently about their work, exploring the potential of blockchain technology to ensure authenticity and create a unique experience for consumers.

The flexibility of a remote working environment also encourages creatives to explore cross-disciplinary projects more freely. Being exposed to various industries and professionals can lead to hybrid ideas and art forms, merging concepts from different fields. Whether it's a graphic designer collaborating with app developers, or a writer working with a game design team, the opportunities for innovation and learning are boundless. Such collaboration not only enriches the creative process but also broadens an artist's skill set and professional horizons.

Additionally, the rise of subscription-based platforms for creatives has paved the way for sustainable income models. By offering exclusive content, such as behind-the-scenes footage, personalized tutorials, or one-on-one sessions, artists can cultivate dedicated fanbases. This model not only provides financial stability but also fosters a deeper connection with audiences. Creatives can thus craft personal brands and storylines that resonate personally with their supporters, encouraging long-term engagement and loyalty.

Beyond individual gain, remote work opens up avenues for creatives to contribute to larger societal narratives and causes. With global connectivity, it's easier than ever to use art as a platform for activism and social change. Creatives can leverage their skills to craft compelling campaigns, raise awareness, and mobilize communities around causes that matter. The digital realm amplifies their voice, ensuring that impactful messages resonate on a larger scale.

Furthermore, the flexibility inherent in remote work environments allows creatives to tailor their work-life balance to better suit personal needs and creative rhythms. Artists, notoriously known for unconventional work hours, can find solace in the autonomous nature of remote work that permits them to tap into their most productive and creative states of mind without the constraints of traditional office hours. This autonomy can lead to more inspired output and a more relaxed approach to the creative process.

In the world of education and skill acquisition, remote working presents artists with the opportunity to grow and evolve continuously. With online courses, webinars, and virtual workshops, creatives are empowered to keep learning and refining their craft. Whether interested in mastering a new software, learning about emerging creative trends, or exploring different artistic techniques, the wealth of available resources is immense. This constant learning environment helps artists stay relevant in their fields and opens up new pathways for artistic exploration.

While opportunities abound, artists must also be cautious of the challenges that accompany the remote landscape. Managing time effectively, maintaining motivation without direct oversight, and navigating the often unpredictable financial terrain of freelance work are critical skills to develop. However, with foresight and planning, these obstacles can become stepping stones towards a fulfilling remote creative career.

Ultimately, the remote work revolution has transformed how artists and creatives operate, providing a canvas rich with possibilities that encourage innovation, collaboration, and personal growth. For those willing to embrace the potential of this new paradigm, the benefits are multifaceted and highly rewarding. Embracing a remote lifestyle enables creatives not just to survive, but to thrive, carving out meaningful and sustainable careers on a global scale.

## Collaboration in Creative Fields

In the world of remote work, creative professionals often stand on the precipice of a unique set of opportunities and challenges. Whether you're an artist, writer, designer, or musician, collaboration remains a core component of your professional success. But how does one maintain the creative spark and synergy when traditional in-person interactions are replaced with digital interfaces?

First, let's consider the core of creative collaboration: inspiration and idea sharing. Establishing a digital landscape where spontaneous inspiration can thrive is essential. Virtual brainstorming sessions can benefit significantly from tools like shared digital whiteboards. These platforms not only capture ideas in real time but also serve as visual repositories that remain accessible for all team members. The ability to revisit and iterate on these visual brainstorms fosters an ongoing cycle of creativity.

Keeping these interactive sessions engaging and productive requires a framework that's both structured and flexible. Begin by setting clear objectives for each meeting. This might seem contrary to the spontaneous ethos of creativity, but having defined outcomes encourages focus and maximizes time efficiency. Encourage team members to go beyond simple verbal exchanges. Sharing visual or auditory materials during meetings can ignite discussions and lead to unexpected breakthroughs.

Within these virtual spaces, maintaining the human element is crucial. Video calls shouldn't just be about work; they can become opportunities to connect on a personal level. Encourage light-hearted interactions, perhaps by starting each meeting with a 'creative warm-up'—this could be as simple as sharing a quick creative exercise or favorite piece of work from the past week. Establish a culture where team members feel comfortable expressing themselves, which fosters an environment of open collaboration.

Another cornerstone of collaboration is feedback—constructive, timely, and compassionate feedback. Remote settings demand a reevaluation of how critique is given and received. Written feedback is common but can often lack the nuanced tone of voice that conveys support alongside criticism. Opt for video or voice messages when possible. Platforms that allow for commenting directly on designs or documents can also mediate this gap, offering a space for more threaded, context-rich discussions.

Given the decentralized nature of remote work, understanding and leveraging time zones is a pivotal challenge. Asynchronous collaboration is not only possible, but it's often required when team members are scattered across the globe. Use collaboration platforms with features that highlight changes, comments, and updates since a member's last log-in, keeping everyone in the loop regardless of their waking hours. This ensures that all contributors can engage with the latest developments without being bound by the limitations of synchronous communication.

Yet, while asynchronous communication is invaluable, the magic often happens in real-time collaboration. Creative professionals should utilize flexible scheduling to allow for overlapping hours—times when all parties can engage live, albeit from different corners of the world. These shared windows can be dedicated to discussions that benefit from immediate feedback and dialogue.

Technology has gifted us with innovative collaboration tools, but the tools themselves need to be tailored to fit the creative process organically. For writers, version control platforms that track changes and comments in documents are incredibly supportive. For visual artists and designers, tools that offer high-resolution image sharing and iteration like cloud-based design programs are indispensable. Musicians might leverage collaboration software that allows real-time editing of tracks. Choosing the right tool often involves considering what software integrates seamlessly into your existing workflows.

The shared digital work-space itself should be viewed as a gallery—dedicated spaces within platforms for housing ongoing projects, drafts, or developmental work. These can act as virtual studios where peers can drop by to offer insights or gain inspiration. Transparency in these areas ensures that each team member feels connected to the broader creative endeavor, promoting a sense of community and shared vision.

In moving creativity to a digital realm, it's essential not to lose sight of the human need for connection. Periodic virtual retreats can serve to bond teams on a deeper level. These events can focus on team-building activities or learning sessions led by team members, enriching skills while fostering camaraderie. The aim is to replicate the essence of an in-person creative residency where ideas pulse, and collaborations unfold naturally.

Lastly, consider the role of leadership in these creative fields. Leaders should act as facilitators of creativity, ensuring that their teams take calculated risks without fear of failure. Encouraging a culture where it's safe to explore unorthodox ideas will frequently yield the most innovative solutions. Remote leaders must also advocate for their teams' needs, ensuring they have access to appropriate tools and mental well-being support.

Creative collaboration in remote settings is a landscape of exciting possibilities when approached with intention and openness. When technology and empathy come together, they build bridges that connect ideas and people across any distance. For remote creatives, the world becomes a canvas—each team member a brushstroke, contributing to a larger masterpiece that continues to evolve with time and creativity.

# Chapter 20: Entrepreneurship for the Remote Worker

Embarking on the entrepreneurial journey is daunting for many, yet for remote workers, it can be a gateway to empowerment and freedom. With flexible hours and the absence of geographical constraints, remote work lays a fertile ground for entrepreneurial pursuits. It's not just about starting a business; it's about crafting a lifestyle that melds one's personal vision with professional prowess. Using skills honed in traditional and remote work settings, today's remote workers can envision and create ventures that might've seemed out of reach a decade ago.

The first step is identifying what drives you. Most successful remote entrepreneurs start by tapping into their passions. Whether it's transforming a hobby into a business or innovating within your professional field, the key is starting with something that lights your fire. This intrinsic motivation becomes your anchor during the inevitable ups and downs. Technology plays a crucial role here, enabling remote entrepreneurs to conduct market research, test their ideas, and reach global audiences without hefty investments. Digital platforms and tools facilitate everything from customer relations to financial management, allowing increased focus on creativity and strategic planning.

Risk is an inherent part of entrepreneurship. For remote workers, it involves pivoting from the perceived stability of employment to the unpredictability of self-driven ventures. Overcoming this fear begins with a solid plan. Crafting a business plan that rigorously tackles potential challenges and clearly outlines objectives is essential. Address questions like: Who are your customers? What value are you offering? How does your venture fit into the current market landscape? A thorough business plan not only serves as a roadmap but also helps secure support from investors or partners.

Networking is another crucial element. While remote work can feel isolating, the digital world offers abundant opportunities for connection. Through online forums, social media, webinars, and virtual conferences, remote workers can collaborate, share insights, and forge partnerships. Building a supportive community around your venture can lead to unexpected opportunities, advice, and even financial backing. Don't hesitate to engage with other entrepreneurs; their experiences can provide valuable lessons that guide your own journey.

Flexibility and adaptability are virtues for the remote entrepreneur. The business landscape can shift quickly, so the ability to pivot and innovate is invaluable. Embrace experimentation, and don't fear failure—it's often through setbacks that the most inventive ideas are refined and realized. Research is critical, yet remaining open to the unexpected and willing to adjust your approach is what will set you apart. This mindset fosters resilience, a key trait for sustaining long-term success in entrepreneurial endeavors.

Finally, it's vital to celebrate successes, no matter how small. Entrepreneurship is a marathon peppered with sprints, and recognizing milestones can bolster motivation and maintain momentum. Remember that the entrepreneurial journey is as much about personal growth as it is about professional accomplishment. The path to entrepreneurship for remote workers is paved with opportunities to redefine work-life balance, challenge conventional norms, and create a future that excites and sustains. Embrace the challenge, dedicate yourself to continuous learning, and let your remote entrepreneurial venture become a reflection of your unique capabilities and vision.

## Starting Your Own Remote Business

So you've been working remotely for a while, and the idea of starting your own business has started to tug at your entrepreneurial spirit. You're not alone. The digital age has not only opened new doors for remote work but also birthed countless opportunities to build a business from anywhere in the world. With the right mindset and tools, what seems daring can become your new reality.

In today's interconnected world, starting a remote business isn't just possible; it's more accessible than ever. Most importantly, the initial capital required is often much lower than traditional brick-and-mortar ventures. The rise of online platforms and digital services means you can test ideas with minimal upfront investment. Whether you're launching a consultancy based on your professional expertise or an e-commerce store selling unique handmade products, the vital first step is validating your business idea. Analyze market needs, get feedback, and refine your concept before diving in.

One of the most significant advantages of a remote business is the freedom to create your own schedule. However, with freedom comes responsibility. Setting boundaries and maintaining a structured routine are critical when you're the one calling the shots. Without the daily commute or office environment, it becomes easy to blur the lines between work and home life. Schedule your day with intention, blending your peak productivity times with breaks that recharge you, preventing burnout before it starts.

Technology is your lifeline as a remote entrepreneur. Choosing the right tools significantly impacts your efficiency and the overall success of your venture. Consider platforms and software that facilitate seamless communication, project management, and customer interaction. Applications like Trello or Slack, for instance, help you stay organized and keep your virtual team on the same page. The right tools not only streamline operations but also enhance your connection with clients or customers, no matter the distance.

Networking plays a crucial role in any business, remote or otherwise. As you step into entrepreneurship, building a strong network should be a priority. Participate in online communities or forums related to your industry. Platforms such as LinkedIn or relevant Facebook groups offer a wealth of interaction opportunities. Attending virtual conferences and webinars can also introduce you to potential partners, clients, or mentors who can guide you forward.

Marketing your remote business effectively is another essential component of success. In a digital-first environment, your online presence is often the first impression you make on potential customers. Craft a compelling brand story and communicate it consistently across your website and social media channels. Understand where your target audience spends their time online and engage them with content that resonates. A solid digital marketing strategy, leveraging social media, SEO, and possibly even paid ads, can place your business in front of the right eyeballs.

As an entrepreneur, you're responsible not only for your business but also for your financial health. Adopting sound financial practices from the onset will serve you well. Budgeting diligently, saving for taxes, and planning for the inevitable ebb and flow of income are foundational practices. Consider consulting with a financial advisor or accountant specializing in small businesses to protect your personal and business assets effectively.

Your progression won't be linear, and that's okay. Challenges and setbacks are inevitable in business but don't let them define you. These experiences are often the best teachers. Embrace a growth mindset, where failure is seen not as an endpoint, but as a stepping stone to improvement. Perseverance and adaptability will guide you through the ups and downs of your entrepreneurial journey.

Moreover, commitment to personal development is key to flourishing in a remote business environment. The constant learning process isn't limited to skill sets related to your business. It also extends to personal growth skills like resilience, emotional intelligence, and self-awareness. Attend workshops, take online courses, or read books that enrich your knowledge. Elevating your skills elevates your business, and staying intellectually curious keeps you at the forefront of your industry.

Perhaps one of the most compelling aspects of starting a remote business is the ability to mold work around your lifestyle. It allows you to redefine success beyond financial gain. It's about creating something that aligns with your values and personal goals. Whether it's spending more time with family, traveling, or contributing to causes you care about, a remote business can be the bridge to a more fulfilling life.

Community and support systems are invaluable to maintaining motivation. Find like-minded entrepreneurs who understand the intricacies of remote work. Sharing experiences can provide encouragement and practical solutions to challenges you face. As much as independence is empowering, collaboration and mentorship can provide insights that solo endeavors might not uncover.

Finally, owning your remote business is not simply about fleeting success; it's about creating lasting impact. As Simon Sinek might argue, start with why. Define a mission that goes beyond profits—a mission that fulfills a greater purpose. This core motivation will sustain your perseverance and resonate with the people you serve.

## Case Studies of Successful Ventures

In the landscape of remote entrepreneurship, inspiring stories of success often rise from the adversity of initial struggles. Consider the case of a tech enthusiast who transformed his small freelance gig into a thriving online consultancy. Initially, he faced the all-too-common challenges of isolation and difficulty in client acquisition. However, through networking in remote work communities and leveraging digital tools, he expanded his reach dramatically. By participating in tech forums and sharing his expertise, he gradually built a reputation that attracted a steady stream of clients from across the globe. This change didn't happen overnight but was a calculated result of consistent effort and a strategic approach to brand positioning.

Another remarkable example is that of a digital nomad who revolutionized her career by launching an online education platform. Recognizing a gap in affordable, high-quality design education, she started with just a laptop and a robust internet connection. Her journey exemplifies the power of merging passion with purpose. Initially providing free workshops, she cultivated a community that eventually turned into paying subscribers. With a strong focus on user feedback and iterative improvements, her platform grew to serve thousands of learners. This case underlines not only the entrepreneurial spirit but also the importance of listening to and evolving with the needs of a community.

The story of a remote wellness coach illustrates the potential of remote entrepreneurship to connect niche markets. After years in a corporate setting, she pivoted to develop a wellness program specifically tailored for remote workers dealing with the stress and solitude of working outside traditional office environments. By leveraging video content, live webinars, and one-on-one coaching sessions, she effectively created a new segment within the wellness industry. Her innovative approach to integrating mindfulness techniques tailored for remote work challenges showcases how addressing specific pain points can be a pivotal strategy for success.

Similarly, we find inspiration in the journey of a couple who turned their love for travel and food into a profitable blog and online store. Combining engaging storytelling with stunning visuals, they attract a dedicated audience of fellow travel enthusiasts. What's more intriguing is how they monetized their blog through diverse revenue streams: partnerships with travel brands, an assortment of creative digital products, and even a subscription-based recipe service. Their success underscores the importance of authenticity and the power of crafting a resonant personal brand that deeply connects with its audience.

Another venture worth exploring is that of a remote-first digital agency that broke away from traditional corporate structures. The founders recognized early on that the future of work was tilting towards flexibility and freedom. By assembling a wholly remote team from various parts of the world, they not only drastically reduced overhead costs but also tapped into a diverse pool of creativity and innovation. This approach not only enabled them to offer competitive pricing to clients but also fostered a company culture where work-life balance was a priority. Their story is a testament to the viability and benefits of remote-first business models.

Let's not overlook the solo entrepreneur who built a software-as-a-service (SaaS) product from his home office. Identifying inefficiencies in project management for remote teams, he developed a tool that addressed these gaps with simplicity and ease of use. Initially bootstrapped and working solo, he focused on refining the product through user feedback while utilizing viral marketing strategies to gain visibility. His relentless focus on product-market fit and building long-term relationships with users resulted in sustained growth and scalability, exemplifying how patience and dedication are key to building successful technology ventures remotely.

Taking a different perspective, consider the ventures that emerged during significant global changes like the COVID-19 pandemic. One small business pivoted effectively when brick-and-mortar operations shut down by going digital almost overnight. Transitioning to an entirely online service model, this company rapidly developed e-commerce capabilities and digital marketing strategies that kept their customer base engaged and active. With adaptability and forward-thinking, they not only survived the tide of change but thrived, demonstrating the importance of flexibility and quick adaptation in uncertain times.

Such ventures also illustrate the pivotal role of effective communication. A common thread in these success stories is the ability to maintain open, constructive channels with stakeholders. The entrepreneurs often embraced digital communication platforms, ensuring their teams and clients remained in sync despite geographical distances. This inclusivity and transparency often led to a mosaic of ideas and solutions that set them apart in competitive markets.

It's crucial to reflect on the empathetic dimension of these stories, where leaders seized the opportunity to address a social or environmental cause while running a profitable venture. For instance, one entrepreneur combined her passion for eco-friendly goods with an e-commerce platform dedicated to sustainably sourced products. Her commitment to sustainability resonated with a growing demographic of conscious consumers, propelling her business to new heights. Her journey teaches us that aligning personal values with business objectives can not only fulfill a market need but also contribute positively to the larger community.

Finally, revisiting the case of freelancers who transformed their freelancing gigs into collaborative startups reveals another layer of success potential in remote entrepreneurship. By using digital collaboration tools and fostering a culture of knowledge sharing, they were able to pool resources, diversify their services, and grow exponentially more than they ever could alone. Their progression from individual contributors to thriving teams offers invaluable insights into the power of collaboration and shared vision.

These case studies illustrate that while the pathways to success can vary widely, the foundational elements of endeavoring into remote entrepreneurship remain consistent. A combination of creativity, adaptability, clarity of vision, and leveraging the power of technology fuels these success stories. Remote work opens horizons and presents unique challenges, but with each challenge comes an opportunity for innovation and growth.

# Chapter 21: The Legal Aspects of Remote Work

In the rapidly evolving landscape of remote work, understanding the legal aspects is not just advisable—it's essential. As work moves away from traditional, centralized offices, the boundaries of what constitutes the "workplace" become blurred, raising numerous legal implications. For remote workers, knowing their rights and responsibilities can make a world of difference. It's about safeguarding your interests while embracing new opportunities.

The shift to remote work necessitates a closer look at worker rights. Each country and sometimes even regions within countries have unique regulations governing remote employment. Understanding these can help you ensure that your rights are not only recognized but respected. Whether it's about overtime pay, health benefits, or safe working conditions, staying informed can prevent potential pitfalls.

Contracts form the foundation of most remote working arrangements and their clarity can determine the success of these engagements. A well-drafted contract can delineate everything from your duties to payment terms, ensuring there is no ambiguity. This is where the importance of contract basics shines through—knowing what to expect and demand in terms of security, both financial and professional. But it's also about fostering trust and transparency between you and your employer or client.

Moreover, with remote work, the concept of jurisdiction might stretch across borders, complicating legal issues. Navigating these waters requires a careful approach, often enlisting legal expertise for complex situations. Here, empathy from employers translates to providing resources and support for contract comprehension. The ultimate goal? To create a workplace—wherever it may be—that's fair and conducive to productivity for all parties involved.

## Understanding Worker Rights

In the dynamic landscape of remote work, understanding worker rights isn't merely beneficial—it's essential. Remote workers, freelancers, and managers are witnessing a transformation in work environments, bringing legal considerations to the forefront. Comprehending these rights helps safeguard your career, maintain fair practices, and protect well-being, forming the bedrock of a thriving remote workforce.

First, let's acknowledge the fact that remote work blurs the line between employee and employer obligations. When a worker's dining room doubles as an office, questions surrounding working hours, overtime, and workplace safety emerge. Each of these elements affects physical and mental health, quality of life, and overall productivity. Knowing where the guidelines sit empowers remote workers to engage confidently with employers about these pressing matters.

The notion of "employment status" can feel more complicated in remote settings. Distinguishing between an independent contractor and an employee isn't just semantics. It dramatically affects your rights, benefits, and responsibilities. For employees, labor laws provide certain protections related to minimum wage, overtime, and non-discrimination, which contractors might not automatically benefit from. Therefore, understanding your employment classification is vital and often requires clarification through employment agreements.

One critical aspect of worker rights in remote settings is understanding how labor laws apply differently in various jurisdictions, especially when working with international teams. Legal frameworks can vary significantly from one country to the next. For instance, while some regions mandate paid leave, others might not, influencing global remote teams' dynamics. Familiarizing yourself with the labor laws applicable to your location—and potentially your employer's location—can avert misunderstandings and ensure compliance.

Moreover, remote workers often express concerns about maintaining work-life balance, which can suffer due to the non-traditional work hours. Fortunately, laws in some countries address this by regulating maximum working hours and mandating rest periods. While these laws mainly apply to employees, remote work's flexible nature can see these lines blurred, often necessitating negotiated solutions. It is crucial to remember that both parties should respect agreed-upon working hours to foster long-term productivity and satisfaction.

In light of recent global events, mental health has become a critical focal point for worker rights discussions. With isolation being a significant challenge for remote workers, many organizations are expanding resources to include mental well-being initiatives. Worker rights increasingly cover occupational health's psychological aspects, requiring employers to consider mental health supportive policies. Remaining informed about these evolving standards aids remote workers in advocating for necessary accommodations and support.

Access to information and transparency remains a cornerstone of informed remote work. Understanding the extent of what you need to know, including expectations on deliverables, performance tracking, and evaluations, can demystify employer expectations. Transparency aids in aligning goals and provides the foundation for a trusting employer-employee relationship. Remember that clear, transparent communication around these aspects is not just a courtesy; it is your right.

The technological essence of remote work brings about cybersecurity concerns. Protecting personal data and ensuring privacy is paramount in this digital age, more so when one's home becomes the workplace. Legal rights include knowing how your employer safeguards your data, what measures are in place to tackle security breaches, and what privacy protections are enforceable. Adopting robust data protection standards not only shields your personal information but fortifies overall company security.

To further solidify your understanding of these rights, education and staying updated are pivotal. Being proactive in learning about the latest worker rights trends ensures that remote workers can adapt and demand a work environment conducive to both productive output and balanced living. Joining professional networks or online communities can provide resources, helping navigate this complex landscape and exchange insights with other remote workers.

Perhaps most importantly, workers should feel empowered to speak up for their rights without the fear of retaliation. Retaliation can undermine the very fabric of worker rights by discouraging open dialogue. Various legal protections exist to prevent this, ensuring workers can express their concerns or grievances safely. Advocacy is a fundamental worker right, fostering a healthy and equitable remote work environment.

As the remote workforce continues to grow, understanding worker rights remains ever more critical. Equipping yourself with knowledge and an awareness of these rights acts as a compass, guiding you through the evolving legal aspects of remote work. This awareness not only protects and empowers you but also contributes towards a thriving, equitable, and vibrant remote work culture.

## Contract Basics

In the dynamic world of remote work, understanding the essentials of contract law isn't just beneficial; it's critical. This understanding serves to protect both employers and remote workers by setting clear expectations and delineating responsibilities. As remote work blurs the traditional lines of employment, the structure of contracts becomes vital in maintaining professionalism, ensuring compliance, and fostering mutual trust. Contracts are the bedrock upon which successful and harmonious work relationships are built, particularly when physical presence isn't part of the equation.

To begin with, the fundamental purpose of a contract in a remote work setting is to legally outline the terms of engagement between parties. This legal document specifies what is expected from both the worker and the employer, addressing key aspects like work hours, deadlines, deliverables, and payment terms. Without such structure, misunderstandings can easily spiral into conflicts that affect productivity and morale. A contract is not just a protective measure but a roadmap to navigate the professional relationship with clarity and confidence.

Equally important is the clarity a contract provides regarding the scope of work. Defining project boundaries helps prevent "scope creep," where additional tasks sneak into a project without formal agreement. For remote workers, this clarity ensures that their workload remains manageable and aligned with initially agreed expectations. For employers, it sets a framework to evaluate performance and output. Clearly articulated roles and objectives lead to efficient workflows and maximize productivity within remote teams.

Another cornerstone of contract basics is the definition and handling of intellectual property (IP) rights. In an age where ideas can travel at the speed of a click, securing intellectual property is indispensable. Contracts must address who owns the work produced and how it can be used or shared. This is especially crucial for freelancers and creatives who deal with unique outputs, such as artwork, software code, or marketing materials. Proper acknowledgment and arrangement of IP rights prevent future disputes and foster a respectful appreciation of each party's contributions.

Contracts must also address the issue of confidentiality and data protection. In a remote setting, sensitive company information is often accessed through various digital platforms. Thus, contracts should include clauses that secure non-disclosure agreements (NDAs) or confidentiality agreements. These agreements protect proprietary information and client data from being misused or leaked. Establishing trust through such measures is paramount in sustaining long-term remote work arrangements.

Pivotal to contract formation is the clear articulation of payment terms. Whether it's hourly, project-based, or a retainer model, knowing when and how compensation will be received is critical for remote workers who often balance multiple gigs. Payment timelines, invoicing procedures, and methods need precise definition to avoid delays and ensure financial stability. Contracts not only secure financial arrangements but also contribute to building trust and reliability.

Moreover, termination clauses are essential components of any remote work contract. They delineate how either party can exit the agreement, including notice periods and any conditions under which the contract may be terminated prematurely. These provisions protect both parties and ensure that even if the collaboration ends, it happens with due process and respect. For remote workers, having clear termination terms offers job security and stability, allowing for informed future planning.

A word about flexibility: while contracts provide structure, they should also allow room for adjustments as needs evolve. Building in flexibility reflects an understanding of the dynamic nature of remote work. Perhaps a project timeline needs an extension, or deliverables may require adaptation. A rigid contract may hamper these shifts, while one with room for negotiation upholds productivity and adaptability. Flexibility in contracts supports an agile work environment that responds well to change.

An often overlooked yet indispensable part of contract formation is dispute resolution mechanisms. Disagreements will arise, but having a pre-defined procedure for resolving issues can save time, money, and professional relationships. Whether it involves mediation, arbitration, or setting jurisdiction for legal proceedings, these measures ensure conflicts are managed efficiently, preserving the integrity and continuity of business operations.

Finally, understanding the legal landscape surrounding contracts is crucial for both remote workers and managers. Awareness of local labor laws, tax obligations, and international work regulations can impact contract terms, especially in cross-border collaborations. Legal consultation becomes a valuable tool in crafting contracts that comply with diverse legal systems, helping avoid potential pitfalls and ensuring alignment with relevant compliance standards.

In essence, contracts are the backbone of remote work relationships. They provide security, clarity, and structure while advocating for respect and mutual benefit. Well-crafted contracts address every aspect of the work relationship, smoothing the journey for remote workers and fostering environments where productivity and creativity can flourish without geographic constraints. Understanding and embracing these contract basics is fundamental to thriving in the evolving landscape of remote work.

# Chapter 22: Navigating Remote Work Policies

Remote work policies shape the framework of how we perform our jobs from afar. They encompass guidelines that help maintain order and support in a virtual environment while granting the flexibility that many value. As remote work sees greater adoption, it's vital to understand these policies not just as constraints, but as integral components meant to enhance efficiency and fairness. Recognizing how these guidelines apply can be a game-changer in experiencing a smooth remote work life.

When diving into remote work agreements, it's essential to get familiar with the specifics of your own contract or policy. These documents often set out the expectations for availability, productivity metrics, and communication routines. Some agreements might specify required working hours or insist on response times within a particular range. Delving into these details proactively allows you to align your work habits and expectations with what's required and excel within those boundaries.

On the flip side, there are legal implications intertwined with remote work policies that you shouldn't overlook. Understanding what these mean for your work rights and privacy is critical. For instance, regulations generally stipulate how companies can monitor performance and handle your data. Familiarizing yourself with these aspects safeguards your rights and clarifies your responsibilities. It also prepares you to advocate effectively if changes in work arrangements occur.

Ultimately, remote work policies, when comprehended and managed effectively, ensure a supportive framework that balances employee flexibility with organizational needs. They help clear ambiguities and provide a greater sense of security for both remote workers and managers. By thoroughly grasping these policies, you empower yourself to not just comply but to leverage them in ways that genuinely enhance your remote work experience.

## Remote Work Agreements

As remote work continues to flourish, the significance of well-crafted remote work agreements can't be overstated. These agreements are much more than mere documents; they're the frameworks that enable a harmonious blend of flexibility and accountability. For remote workers, freelancers, and managers, these agreements help anchor the dynamic world of decentralized employment. They clarify roles, set expectations, and serve as a reference point for both parties.

Creating a comprehensive remote work agreement is both a practical and strategic endeavor. It entails a thorough understanding of the roles involved and the specific tasks required. It should serve as a guide, charting out the responsibilities of both the remote worker and the employer. This agreement needs to stand as a beacon, illuminating the path forward and minimizing ambiguity. Establishing these clear expectations from the beginning can prevent misunderstandings down the road.

The process of developing a remote work agreement should begin with an open conversation between the employer and employee or contractor. This dialogue should aim to forge a mutual understanding of project scopes, deliverables, and deadlines. Clear communication at this stage fosters trust and allows both parties to express their needs and expectations transparently. This discussion lays the groundwork for a productive working relationship.

Key components of a robust remote work agreement include details about work hours, communication protocols, and performance metrics. Defining work hours, while allowing for flexibility, ensures that both parties have a consistent schedule to rely upon. It's about balancing autonomy with the need for reliability. Communication protocols help maintain connectivity. Whether through email, instant messaging, or video calls, defining these tools can prevent unnecessary delays and ensure that everyone is on the same page.

Performance metrics are another crucial element of the agreement. These metrics should be crafted to offer meaningful insights into the worker's effectiveness without becoming overly burdensome. They should encourage high performance without micromanaging. Put simply, they should be a compass, guiding the worker towards objective achievements while providing the employer with a fair measure of progress.

Remote work agreements should also consider the tools and resources required for success. Employers need to ensure that their remote workers have access to all necessary technology and support. This includes providing software licenses, access to remote servers, or any tools essential to completing tasks efficiently. By doing so, employers can remove barriers that might hinder productivity.

A critical aspect of any remote work agreement is the inclusion of clauses related to data security and confidentiality. Given the increasingly digital nature of remote work, safeguarding sensitive information is paramount. An agreement should specify the measures to protect data and outline the steps one should take in the event of a data breach. These clauses reassure both parties that their information is secure.

Flexibility is a key advantage of remote work, and agreements can accommodate this advantage by including provisions for adapting to change. Roles can evolve and project priorities can shift; therefore, contracts that allow for periodic reviews will remain relevant and effective. Such clauses not only recognize the dynamic nature of remote work but also facilitate ongoing communication and adjustment between the worker and the employer.

In addition to the practical terms, remote work agreements should also consider cultural and interpersonal aspects. Remote work often involves diverse teams from different cultural backgrounds, and acknowledging these differences in the agreement can enhance team cohesion. Addressing how cultural nuances impact communication can foster a more inclusive and empathetic work environment.

Developing effective remote work agreements is not just about policy, it's about understanding the human element. Empathy must thread through these documents, recognizing the challenges and benefits remote workers and employers experience. By building agreements grounded in empathy, all parties can work in environments that are both productive and supportive.

Finally, while remote work agreements are fundamental, they should not be static. As the remote work landscape evolves, so too should these agreements. Regular reviews and updates are essential to ensure they remain relevant and beneficial. By maintaining this living document approach, remote work agreements can continue to serve as a cornerstone of successful remote work relationships.

## Legal Implications

Navigating the legal implications of remote work policies requires a thorough understanding of various aspects, ranging from employment laws to data protection regulations. Remote work offers unparalleled flexibility, but it also brings complex legal landscapes that remote workers and managers must traverse with care. The journey begins with grasping the intricacies of employment status and agreements, laying the foundations for a healthy and compliant working relationship.

The first step in addressing legal implications is understanding the classification of remote workers. Are they independent contractors or employees? The determination of this status affects everything from tax obligations to benefits eligibility. It's crucial for both parties to have clarity on this distinction to avoid misunderstanding and potential disputes. Often, remote workers might find themselves classified as independent contractors, which generally means more freedom but less security in terms of workplace rights. On the other hand, employees are protected by labor laws but may have less flexibility. Knowing where you stand helps in determining rights and responsibilities, safeguarding interests, and ensuring compliance with applicable laws.

A robust remote work agreement is vital. It acts as a formal acknowledgment of the terms and conditions under which remote work is conducted. These agreements often include specifics about work hours, deliverables, communication expectations, and technology usage. They serve as a reference point should disagreements arise, providing clarity and reducing potential legal tensions. Clarity here isn't just practical—it's protective. Both parties should engage legal professionals when necessary to draft and review such agreements to ensure all bases are covered and neither party is disadvantaged.

Data protection has emerged as a critical legal consideration in remote work environments. With a decentralized workforce, sensitive company and client data are increasingly at risk of breaches. Laws such as the General Data Protection Regulation (GDPR) in Europe and the California Consumer Privacy Act (CCPA) in the United States lay out stringent guidelines for data handling and privacy. Remote workers need to be aware of these legal standards, fostering a secure work environment through best practices such as encryption, regular software updates, and secure communication channels. Companies must also provide training and tools to help remote employees comply with data protection laws.

Intellectual property rights can become particularly fuzzy in remote work situations. When working from home, the line between personal and professional becomes blurred, raising questions about ownership and use of work material and tools. Employers should outline intellectual property rights clearly in contracts, specifying ownership of any products, ideas, or materials developed during work hours and with company resources. Remote workers, meanwhile, should be proactive in understanding these clauses to protect their own creative inputs.

International remote work brings another layer of legal complexity. Working across borders introduces varied jurisdictional laws that can affect remote work agreements and operations—from taxation to employment laws. Companies and remote workers need to be diligent in understanding which jurisdiction's laws apply and how to comply with them. This includes recognizing different tax obligations when working internationally and ensuring compliance to avoid hefty penalties. Sometimes, companies might need to engage legal counsel specializing in international employment law to navigate these waters effectively.

The legal implications extend to health and safety regulations, which traditionally pertained to physical office spaces but are now increasingly relevant in home offices. Remote workers might be surprised to learn that health and safety laws can apply to them at home, requiring employers to ensure that home working conditions are safe and ergonomically sound. Companies should offer guidance and perhaps financial assistance for setting up safe workspaces, focusing on ergonomics to minimize risk of injury. Workers must take responsibility too, ensuring their home setup complies with these regulations.

Additionally, discrimination and equal treatment laws still apply in remote work settings, requiring employers to ensure fairness and equality irrespective of where their employees are located. Remote workers should be vigilant about their rights, ensuring they are not overlooked for promotions or opportunities due to the physical distance from their company's headquarters.

In essence, the legal framework around remote work is not static but ever-evolving in response to changes in how we define "workplaces" and "workforces." Companies and remote workers alike must remain adaptable, informed, and proactive in understanding these implications, regularly revisiting their agreements and practices to ensure ongoing compliance. By doing this, they build not just legally sound, but also trust-filled and productive remote work environments that empower everyone involved to thrive.

# Chapter 23: Remote Work Across Time Zones

Working remotely across time zones can feel like conducting an orchestra with musicians in different cities. Yet, with the right strategies, it's possible to create harmony instead of discord. In today's global workspace, flexibility becomes our greatest ally. Understanding the nature of time zones is essential; it goes beyond simple arithmetic. It requires empathy and an appreciation for diverse work-life balances. The sun may start setting for one teammate as another is just starting their day. This compels us to find creative solutions that respect both productivity and personal lives.

Coordinating international teams is more art than science. It starts with understanding the specific needs and preferences of each team member. Maybe your marketing expert finds their peak creativity in the early morning, while your developer hits their stride after sundown. Find common ground by prioritizing transparency and frequent communication, which ensures everyone stays on the same page despite the distance. Use collaboration tools that offer seamless conversation threads and file sharing, making sure everyone feels equally connected.

Timing and scheduling become the backbone of successful remote operations. Leverage technology to keep track of time zone differences and employ scheduling apps to accommodate everyone's calendar. Encourage teams to establish core hours—a window when everyone is expected to be online. This reduces guesswork and enables spontaneous ideas to flourish during overlapping times. It's important to be flexible, recognizing that rigid schedules can strain productivity and relationships. Acknowledging each person's unique rhythms and integrating them into workflows can boost morale and efficiency.

The challenges are real but so are the rewards of effectively managing remote teams across time zones. It's about finding what works, experimenting, and iterating as you go, remembering that every team is unique. By fostering an environment that thrives on clarity and mutual respect, remote work across time zones transforms from a complex puzzle into a tapestry of global collaboration.

# Coordinating International Teams

As remote work becomes more common, the challenge of coordinating international teams grows in importance. Bringing together a diverse group from various time zones offers a wealth of perspectives and ideas, yet it also presents unique obstacles. This doesn't mean it's an insurmountable task; rather, it's an opportunity to refine collaboration strategies and nurture a more connected and efficient team.

A dynamic and empathetic approach can make collaboration across time zones smoother. Start by understanding each team member's time zone as a foundation. This not only shows respect for everyone's schedules but also helps in planning meetings and deadlines. Tools like world clocks or scheduling software can aid in visualizing overlaps and gaps in the team's work hours, reducing frustration around scheduling.

Communication is essential when crossing time zones. Beyond scheduling, understanding cultural nuances can facilitate smoother interactions. While some team members might prefer direct communication, others might find indirect approaches more comfortable. Encourage an open dialogue about these preferences, as they can vary significantly and affect overall team dynamics.

## Embracing Asynchronous Communication

It's crucial to empower teams by embracing asynchronous communication. Not everything requires immediate responses or real-time meetings. Platforms that allow threaded discussions, such as project management tools or team forums, ensure everyone can contribute without the pressure of being "on call" constantly. This not only accommodates different time zones but fosters deeper, more thoughtful contributions, as team members can engage with the material at their own pace.

To make asynchronous work efficient, ensure that instructions and expected outcomes are clear and documented. Relying on written communication allows everyone to revisit and review the task at hand, minimizing misunderstandings that might arise due to time lapses. Regularly update and organize shared documents, so everyone stays on the same page, quite literally.

Harnessing collaboration platforms is another tactic to unify international teams. Choose platforms that allow for task management, document sharing, and real-time messaging. Such tools bridge geographical gaps and create a virtual workspace where everyone has equal access to information and communication channels. Yet, choosing the right platform isn't the end of the journey—it's essential to provide training and make these tools a natural part of the workflow.

## Building Trust and Camaraderie

Trust-building activities are often overlooked when teams work remotely across borders. But fostering personal connections can significantly enhance collaboration. Simple actions, like scheduling regular virtual coffee breaks or team-building exercises, can develop rapport and understanding. Cameras on or off, the aim is to create a space where team members feel comfortable sharing insights and experiences beyond work.

Shared projects that require pairs or small groups to collaborate can also strengthen interpersonal relationships within the team. Getting to know each other's strengths and working styles can build a network of support that stretches across time zones, leading to a more resilient team overall.

Regular feedback contributes to a positive team environment as well. It helps create a culture of closure where projects are completed, and lessons learned without unnecessary stress. Implement feedback sessions that focus on workflow improvement rather than criticism. These should be viewed as opportunities for growth—a chance for the whole team to learn from both successes and missteps.

**Managing Meetings and Deadlines**

Meetings that span multiple time zones must be planned with care. While some compromise is inevitable, strive for equity so no single team's working hours are consistently disrupted. Distribute the timing of meetings fairly, recognizing that fair doesn't always mean equal. Sometimes, rotating meeting times can help balance the inconvenience among team members.

The urgency of deadlines should be considered thoughtfully. When setting deadlines, recognize that a workday's end varies across the globe. Whenever possible, allow buffers for time zone differences, ensuring that no one is forced to work unsociable hours to meet a timeline. Agile methodologies often work well in this setting, as they can provide flexibility that accounts for diverse schedules.

Empower team members to manage their tasks independently by setting clear priorities. This not only boosts morale but also leverages the autonomy that remote work affords. Give them the resources they need to succeed, including the freedom to organize their work days in a way that aligns with their peak productivity times. Expectations should be result-oriented rather than time-oriented, emphasizing output over the hours logged.

Ultimately, the goal is to cultivate a culture that values inclusivity, flexibility, and empathy. A team spread across different time zones can be just as cohesive and efficient as one located in a single office, provided that the nuances of remote work are respected and integrated thoughtfully into every interaction. With the right strategies, coordinating international teams does more than bridge physical distances; it strengthens organizational coherence and innovation.

## Timing and Scheduling Best Practices

As the world becomes smaller, remote work offers the unprecedented ability to collaborate with teams across different time zones. However, this geographical flexibility also introduces unique timing and scheduling challenges. Effectively managing these requires a blend of strategy, empathy, and the clever use of digital tools, ensuring that teams remain productive and connected despite the miles that separate them.

At the heart of effective scheduling lies an understanding of time zone differences. It's not just about knowing who is where but also appreciating how these differences impact work patterns and productivity. For remote workers and managers alike, it's crucial to not only recognize the gaps but also to bridge them thoughtfully. This might mean scheduling important meetings during overlapping work hours or adopting asynchronous communication methods to accommodate everyone's availability.

Effective scheduling in a remote setting begins with transparency. Shared calendars become indispensable tools. They provide a visual representation of each team member's work hours, helping schedule meetings at times that are mutually convenient. When everyone sees the complete picture, it becomes easier to plan around commitments or routine events, like school pickups or after-work activities, thereby respecting personal time and reducing unnecessary stress.

But it's not all about technology. There's a human aspect we can't ignore. Encouraging open conversations about time preferences and constraints can help optimize schedules even further. When team members feel comfortable expressing when they're most productive or when they need flexible hours, managers can tailor schedules to enhance efficiency and employee satisfaction. Sometimes, it's the conversations around scheduling that reveal the most about team dynamics and individual preferences.

There's value in regular rhythms. Teams may find it helpful to establish standard times for recurring meetings. This consistency not only simplifies planning but also builds routine into the virtual environment, which can otherwise feel fluid and unpredictable. While spontaneous meetings have their place, relying too heavily on them can disrupt personal and professional balance.

In distributed teams, asynchronous work becomes vital. It's not just about filling time gaps but leveraging them. Crafting thoughtful messages with all the necessary context can help colleagues in different time zones respond effectively when they start their day. Consider the power of detailed status updates, recorded video messages, or comprehensive emails — these become the asynchronous lifeline of a team.

One of the key best practices is investing in tools that track availability across time zones. These could range from world clock apps to more sophisticated solutions integrated within team communication platforms that automatically display each person's local time during interactions. Such technology minimizes confusion and helps streamline routine scheduling tasks, leaving more energy for the work itself.

Another effective strategy is to rotate meeting times. If a weekly meeting always falls at inconvenient times for certain team members, consider rotating it. By doing so, everyone sacrifices fairly, and no single person consistently bears the brunt of time zone inconvenience. This practice fosters a sense of equality and solidarity within the team.

Flexibility is indispensable. Sometimes, the best-laid plans will have to accommodate unexpected shifts, either in priorities or in personal schedules. Encouraging flexibility and adaptability helps teams maintain high morale and productivity even when work schedules need to be adjusted unexpectedly. It's all about creating an environment where flexibility is understood as a mutual benefit, not a burden.

Ultimately, successful scheduling for remote work involves striking a balance between structure and flexibility. The balance is essential because it respects team members' time while ensuring that critical tasks don't fall through the cracks. Clear guidelines combined with personal responsibility ensure that team members are synchronized, no matter where they are.

Building and sustaining trust is the glue that holds remote teams together. Trust that every team member will manage their time wisely, trust in everyone's commitment to shared goals, and trust that no one will take advantage of the collective flexibility. When trust is present, scheduling is less of a chore and more of a collaborative effort towards achieving common objectives.

Remember, as much as timing and scheduling are about calendars and clocks, they are also about respect and empathy. Understand that each individual operates within their unique context. Giving space for personal responsibilities and acknowledging the diverse work environments across time zones can dramatically enhance team cohesion and operational efficiency.

By intentionally applying these best practices, remote teams position themselves to leverage their diverse geographical presence as a unique strength rather than a logistical challenge. When teams conscientiously navigate the complexities of scheduling across time zones, they not only do good work but create an inclusive and supportive work culture that thrives on connection and collaboration.

# Chapter 24: Advancing Your Career Remotely

As the landscape of work shifts, advancing your career remotely has become not just a possibility, but an exciting reality. Embracing this change requires a proactive approach, where opportunities for growth and leadership are not just handed to you but are actively pursued. Many remote workers find that their path to advancement is less about traditional face-time and more about delivering exceptional results, honing specialized skills, and demonstrating invaluable adaptability.

Start by setting clear personal and professional goals. Defining your objectives provides a roadmap for your journey, allowing you to track your achievements and identify areas needing improvement. This clarity of direction is empowering, turning remote work from a static routine into a dynamic career-building exercise. Remember, visibility in a remote setting often correlates with the quality of work you deliver and your communication skills. Consistently pitch your ideas, contribute to team discussions, and keep your managers informed of your work progress.

Seek out growth opportunities by leveraging technology to connect with mentors and participate in webinars, workshops, and conferences. Remote work doesn't limit your access to industry leaders and innovators; in fact, it often broadens it. Cultivating relationships with mentors can lead to a deeper understanding of industry trends and expose you to new opportunities. These engagements not only enhance your skill set but also add to your professional narrative, giving you an edge in career advancement.

Building a career remotely also means being prepared to switch gears or pivot into new roles when opportunities arise. This agility comes from continuous learning and staying attuned to the evolving needs of the industry. Expand your horizons by acquiring new competencies through online courses or certifications relevant to your field. By doing so, you remain not only competitive but indispensable.

In conclusion, advancing your career remotely involves a strategic blend of self-motivation, ongoing development, and fearless communication. It's about setting the vision for your future, crafting the network that supports it, and adapting your skills to match an ever-changing market. The digital world is your stage, and your ability to navigate it determines your path forward.

## Promotions and Growth Opportunities

In the evolving landscape of remote work, the path to career advancement may seem as shifting as the digital sand beneath our feet. But just as we've learned to navigate online meetings and virtual collaboration, so too can we master the art of advancing our careers remotely. Whether you're a freelancer charting your own course or part of a dispersed team, grasping the threads of growth opportunities is within your reach. By proactively engaging with your career development, you can not only find the golden moments for promotion but transform your role from a mere job into a platform for significant impact and personal fulfillment.

Firstly, let's dispel the myth that visibility takes a hit when you're operating remotely. On the contrary, remote work offers unique avenues to make your accomplishments shine. The key is to position yourself as a proactive problem-solver and a dependable team player. Consistently delivering high-quality work, coupled with making your achievements known through effective communication, can set you apart. Instead of waiting for annual reviews, periodically share your successes, whether it's through dedicated updates to your manager or presenting insights during team meetings. This not only highlights your contributions but also keeps you on their radar. In a remote setting, self-promotion is not just beneficial—it's essential.

Consider the vast benefits of engaging in continuous learning and skill development. The world of online courses opens up as a valuable resource, offering credentials and training that can significantly enhance your skill set. Think of education as a strategic investment; it can set you apart and prepare you for roles you might aspire to in the future. Employers are more likely to promote individuals who show initiative and commitment to their own growth. While mastering a new technology or coding language can certainly boost your qualifications, so too can developing soft skills such as leadership, communication, and emotional intelligence, which are critical in remote settings.

Networking is not confined to physical spaces. Embracing virtual networking can be a powerful means of uncovering new opportunities. Participate in online industry forums, webinars, and remote-friendly conferences. Here, you can meet professionals who might guide you, partner with you, or even present you with your next job opportunity. Cultivating relationships within your industry is vital; they can lead to mentorships and open broader channels for your career that extend beyond your current role. Keep in mind that building genuine relationships is about giving as much as receiving—offer your support, expertise, or insights where you can.

Achieving a promotion in a remote environment also requires demonstrating leadership capabilities, even if you're not in a formal leadership role. Lead by example in collaboration, offer constructive feedback, and demonstrate initiative by volunteering for challenging projects. Building a reputation as someone who can lead a remote team effectively will naturally position you for advancement. Every project is a platform to showcase strategic thinking and adaptability—qualities that are highly valued in remote work.

Your digital presence is as crucial as your in-office demeanor once was. Ensure that your online professional profiles are up-to-date and reflect your current achievements and aspirations. Platforms like LinkedIn are great for showcasing your professional journey, enabling recruiters and industry peers to see your growth and potential. Think of your online presence not just as a resume but as a dynamic portfolio that captures your evolving career narrative.

Lastly, never underestimate the power of seeking feedback. Regularly ask for evaluations from your managers and peers to understand how you're perceived and where you can improve. Constructive criticism can be a catalyst for growth, helping you pinpoint skills or habits to develop further. An openness to feedback can demonstrate your commitment to continuous improvement and underscore your readiness for greater responsibilities.

Remote advancement isn't just about climbing the ladder; it's about rediscovering your career path in a landscape filled with opportunities. The flexibility of remote work can be a powerful ally in creating a balance that supports both professional and personal growth. By setting clear goals, adopting a proactive approach, and continuously investing in your development, you carve a path to not only career success but to becoming a more fulfilled professional in today's interconnected world.

## Building a Remote Career Path

Crafting a successful career isn't limited to the confines of a traditional office anymore. The digital age presents an open door for remote workers to sculpt their own professional trajectories. If you're ready to pioneer your career path from your home office, co-working space, or the local coffee shop, a structured approach is essential. While remote work offers unprecedented flexibility, it demands a proactive strategy to ensure continuous growth and advancement.

Firstly, envision where you want to be in the next five, ten, or even twenty years. Visualizing your end goals can provide the roadmap needed to guide your career choices. This could involve climbing the corporate ladder in a remote-friendly company or perhaps acquiring new skills that open doors to fresh opportunities. Clearly defining your aspirations allows you to set tangible milestones and create a strategic plan to achieve them.

Strategic skill development is crucial for building a remote career path. The fast pace of technological change means continuous learning should be a constant in your career plan. Identify the skills that are in demand in your industry and invest time in acquiring them. Online courses, webinars, and virtual workshops are readily accessible for honing these skills. Learning shouldn't be viewed as a disruptive task but rather as a catalyst for innovation and personal growth.

Equally important is building a professional network that extends beyond geographical boundaries. Networking in a remote work environment may look different, but it's no less vital. Join virtual industry groups, participate in online forums, and attend webinars where you can meet like-minded professionals. Cultivating these relationships can lead to mentorship opportunities, collaborative projects, and even job offers.

Remember, showcasing your achievements is integral to career advancement in any setting, especially in the remote workspace. Keep an updated portfolio that highlights your work and the impact it has had on your projects or clients. Visibility, even from afar, is key in making sure your achievements are recognized by peers and superiors alike. Regularly check in with your supervisors or clients to discuss your contributions and future goals.

Don't shy away from seeking new responsibilities or projects that challenge your existing skills. When you're no longer present in a physical office, you need to actively communicate your willingness and readiness to take on new challenges. This initiative can drive career growth and signal to your managers that you're ready for a bigger role. Be prepared to step out of your comfort zone and embrace tasks that push the boundaries of your capabilities.

Balancing specialization and diversification can also play a significant role in career development. While it's beneficial to be an expert in a particular field, having a broad skill set can make you more versatile and adaptable. This dual approach can open doors to various career paths, ensuring you're not only valuable but indispensable to your team or clients.

The path to career advancement remotely isn't without hurdles. Staying motivated without the traditional office structure can be tough. However, setting regular, realistic goals can help maintain momentum. Break down larger objectives into smaller, more manageable tasks, and reward yourself for achieving them. This method keeps you focused and driven, converting large projects into a series of achievable steps.

Emotional intelligence and communication skills are often highlighted as essential in remote working environments. While technical skills form the foundation of any career, how you manage relationships and communicate can substantially influence your professional growth. Practicing empathy and actively listening during virtual meetings enable stronger connections, fostering a positive remote work culture. When team members feel heard and valued, team cohesion and productivity rise.

In addition, evaluating your progress is essential in a remote career path. Regular self-assessment allows you to recognize what works and what doesn't, ensuring you're on the right track to meet your goals. Periodic evaluations also help in identifying gaps in skills or experience that need to be addressed.

Finally, embrace the myriad possibilities that remote work brings. It offers the opportunity to collaborate globally, innovate freely, and maintain a work-life balance that suits your personal circumstances. Establishing a remote career path isn't just about reaching an endpoint but enjoying the journey, learning, and growing with each experience.

Building a remote career path is both a challenge and an opportunity. It's about proactively taking charge, setting clear goals, and harnessing the flexibility offered by a remote work environment. By investing in yourself and your network, maintaining visibility, and continually reassessing your goals, you set the stage for a fulfilling and prosperous career in the virtual world.

# Chapter 25: Emergency Preparedness for Remote Workers

In the fast-moving world of remote work, where agility and independence are celebrated, it's crucial to recognize that emergencies can strike regardless of your location. These disruptions could range from natural disasters to unexpected power outages or even personal emergencies. As remote workers, being prepared helps ensure your workflow remains unaffected and your peace of mind intact.

A robust contingency plan is the cornerstone of emergency preparedness. Start by identifying potential risks that could disrupt your work. Is your internet connection reliable? What will you do if you experience a prolonged outage? Consider investing in a portable hotspot or finding nearby coworking spaces that might serve as a backup. A simple step like this keeps you connected and productive even when your usual setup fails you.

Another vital aspect of preparedness is developing a comprehensive communication strategy. Ensure you have a list of alternative channels to reach your team and clients if your primary modes of communication go down. This could involve having a secondary device ready or apps that allow messaging without internet access. Keeping lines open fosters a sense of stability and reassurance among your colleagues and clients during chaos.

Beyond connectivity, staying organized amidst an emergency is key. Digital backups of essential documents safeguard you against data loss. Utilize cloud storage solutions to keep your vital work accessible from any device. If you've got company files to manage, ensure they are backed up to a secure location regularly. This habit not only facilitates seamless transitions during emergencies but also supports your everyday efficiency.

Furthermore, being adaptable to unexpected changes can be a game-changer. Cultivating flexibility in your work methods empowers you to switch gears effortlessly. Maybe your workspace becomes uninhabitable temporarily. In such cases, being open to working from a café, library, or even a relative's place can be beneficial. Sometimes, it even means adjusting your work hours slightly to accommodate a schedule thrown off by unforeseen events.

It's essential to remember that preparedness extends beyond resources and technology. Mental readiness plays a critical role too. Building resilience will help you maintain your well-being during an emergency. Practice stress-relief techniques and prioritize self-care, even when things seem manageable. Regularly reflecting on past experiences also gives you insights into how you can better handle future crises.

Emergency preparedness isn't about expecting the worst; it's about planning for it so you can focus on doing your best work, regardless of the circumstances. By taking proactive steps to safeguard your operations and mental health, you'll prove that remote workers can tackle any challenge the world throws their way. After all, being prepared isn't just a safety net—it's a powerful tool that sustains your journey in the ever-evolving landscape of remote work.

## Contingency Planning

In the world of remote work, contingency planning isn't just a luxury—it's a necessity. Imagine waking up to a morning where a power outage has knocked out your internet, or you're informed of a critical software update that decides to malfunction mid-project. These scenarios can send pulses racing, especially when deadlines loom. It's crucial to have robust plans in place to avoid these potential pitfalls, ensuring a seamless work experience no matter what the day throws your way.

At the foundation of every solid contingency plan is the anticipation of potential disruptions. Start by identifying primary risks, such as technical failures, personal emergencies, or connectivity issues. Make a list, get specific, and prioritize these risks by likelihood and impact. Understanding your vulnerabilities allows you to prepare thoughtfully and efficiently. After narrowing down your risks, develop specific strategies or solutions for each scenario. This process involves thinking critically about what resources are needed and how to deploy them when challenges arise.

Take, for instance, the ever-dreaded internet outage. A savvy remote worker might have a backup plan involving a mobile hotspot or access to a nearby co-working space to minimize downtime. Similarly, if your laptop suddenly crashes, having access to a cloud backup ensures that work can resume on another device without losing valuable time or data. Investing in reliable technology and software services, as well as maintaining regular updates, can mitigate these technical hiccups. It's all about being proactive rather than reactive.

Perhaps one of the more underestimated aspects of contingency planning is effective communication. Establish clear communication channels and protocols for how to notify teammates and managers quickly if something disrupts the workflow. This might involve a dedicated messaging platform or an emergency contact method. Regular check-ins can also help identify potential issues before they escalate. Keeping everyone in the loop helps maintain a strong team dynamic, even when plans don't go accordingly.

Let's not overlook the importance of personal emergencies—those unexpected life events that require your immediate attention. Having an informed and flexible team can make all the difference. Consider creating a buddy system where colleagues can cover for each other or having a clearly documented workflow that ensures that tasks can be resumed or handed over with minimal interruption. Designating responsibilities in advance can greatly alleviate stress and aid business continuity.

Fluidity is a hallmark of effective contingency plans. Work environments change, technologies evolve, and new risks emerge. Regularly review and update your contingency plans to address these shifts. Conduct mock drills or hypothetical scenarios within your team to ensure everyone is familiarized with their roles in an emergency. This constant refinement process strengthens your plan and ensures it stays relevant. Remember, a plan that isn't adapted over time can quickly become obsolete.

Your workspace setup plays a pivotal role in contingency planning as well. Design your home office such that it leverages both flexibility and functionality. Consider dual monitors or portable setups that allow you to work from different locations with ease. Ensuring you have a range of rechargeable devices or even a power bank can keep you going through unforeseen circumstances. A well-equipped workspace prepares you for seamless transitions and reduces the anxiety when faced with a sudden change.

Additionally, think of contingency planning as another form of personal branding. It shows reliability, foresight, and professionalism. In a remote setting, where trust is built on the ability to deliver consistently, having these plans in place boosts not only your confidence but your credibility amongst peers and supervisors. It's a way of saying, "I've thought ahead, and I've got this." In times of turbulence, this mindset is just what keeps the ship steady.

Finally, keep an emotional backup plan ready. Remote work often blurs personal and professional boundaries, which can lead to stress in unforeseen circumstances. Mindfulness practices, scheduled breaks, or wellness routines serve as personal contingency measures to help maintain mental calm. Don't underestimate the power of reaching out—whether to a friend, mentor, or a professional—to navigate these challenges together. After all, resilience is also built on self-compassion and understanding your limits.

Remote work brings unprecedented freedom and flexibility, yet it also demands a level of preparedness and resilience. Thoughtful contingency planning is how you navigate unpredictability with grace, minimizing disruptions and maximizing productivity. As you chart this course, remember that planning isn't about eliminating all risks but about preparing for them. Equipped with well-laid plans, you aren't just surviving remote work. You're thriving in it, turning potential setbacks into stepping stones for success.

## Adapting to Unexpected Changes

When we dive into the world of remote work, one truth stands out: change is omnipresent. Whether it's a sudden shift in project timelines, an unanticipated technology breakdown, or a global event that upheaves the way we work, flexibility is vital. The hallmark of a successful remote worker lies not just in anticipating changes but in adapting and thriving amidst them.

Remote workers enjoy numerous benefits, like flexible schedules and the comfort of home offices. However, these perks come with their own set of challenges, particularly the need for quick adaptation to unforeseen circumstances. The transition to remote work itself was a significant change for many, forcing adaptations in work styles, communication methods, and time management strategies. Embracing this mindset allows remote workers to be resilient when faced with the unexpected.

**Expect the Unexpected**: One of the core tenets of adaptability is expecting the unexpected. In a decentralized work environment, things don't always go as planned. Internet outages, software crashes, or even a family emergency can interrupt your workday without warning. Savvy remote workers keep backup plans in place. This might mean having an offline task list for when your internet goes down or having a secondary device at the ready should your primary one fail. It's about building a safety net that ensures productivity even when things don't go your way.

Regularly updating your work contingency plans is crucial. It's not just about how you'll continue working if your Wifi goes out; it's about being prepared for multiple scenarios. Consider potential hurdles specific to your job and workspace. What if your primary communication tool fails? Do you have an alternative in place? These are questions that, when answered in advance, can minimize stress and maximize problem-solving speed when difficulties arise.

Technology, which has empowered the rise of remote work, can also be unpredictable. This means more time should be invested in understanding the tools at your disposal. Dive deeper into those often overlooked settings in your software applications and learn their offline capabilities. Equip yourself with both user knowledge and technical troubleshooting skills. This proactive learning transforms you into a more independent worker and builds an essential skill set in today's digital age.

**Mindset and Agility**: Adaptability starts with a flexible mindset. Approach challenges with a solution-oriented outlook rather than a defeatist one. Those who view problems as opportunities for growth are better positioned to pivot and adapt. In moments of uncertainty, maintaining composure and clarity of thought becomes an advantage. You can't predict every crisis, but you can control how you respond to it.

The importance of a positive, adaptive mindset extends beyond mere personal growth; it influences your professional image. Employers and clients observe how you handle adversity. Demonstrating composure and quick problem-solving in challenging situations not only underscores your reliability but also opens avenues for greater responsibilities and leadership roles.

**Communication and Collaboration**: Don't underestimate the role of communication in successfully adapting to changes. Foster open lines of communication with your team and create a culture of transparency. When everyone is aware of existing or potential issues, collaborative problem-solving is faster and more effective. This open dialogue should also emphasize feedback, which is a valuable tool for continuous improvement and adaptation.

Working remotely can sometimes feel isolating, especially when everything goes awry. Engaging in regular check-ins with your team, using both digital platforms and occasional face-to-face meetings if possible, fosters a sense of community and shared purpose. This network can provide support during challenging times and serve as a resource for innovative solutions that you may not have considered.

**Personal Effectiveness**: On an individual level, continuously refining your skills enhances your ability to pivot when new challenges arise. Remote work offers the unique opportunity to incorporate learning directly into your workflow. Set aside time regularly to update your skills, delve into new tools, and reflect on your work performance. Incorporating mechanisms like self-assessment and peer reviews ensures that you're always prepared for the next big shift, even if you don't know what that shift might be.

Additionally, personal well-being plays a critical role in adaptability. Ensuring you're physically and mentally fit doesn't just enhance productivity; it also boosts your resilience against unexpected changes. Routine exercise, healthy eating habits, and adequate breaks during work create an equilibrium that makes it easier to handle disruptions without being overwhelmed.

Organization can be a remote worker's best friend when adapting to change. Keeping an organized workspace and a structured routine allows you to focus quickly on problem-solving instead of losing time to disorganization. Use digital tools to track your tasks and deadlines, but also maintain some form of a physical planner for those times when digital access is limited.

In conclusion, the art of adapting to unexpected changes in remote work requires a blend of preparation, mindset agility, effective communication, and personal development. It's about viewing each unexpected event not as a barrier but as a stepping stone towards resilience and growth. Embrace this ethos, and you'll find yourself not just surviving in remote work, but thriving and inspiring others in the process.

# Conclusion

As we draw to the close of this comprehensive guide on remote work, it's crucial to reflect on the transformative journey that remote work represents. This lifestyle, once a luxury, has now become a cornerstone of modern employment, offering both unique challenges and exceptional opportunities. Through the pages of this book, we've explored the vast landscape of working remotely, from setting up your virtual office to navigating the complexities of international collaboration.

Remote work, at its heart, grants us the freedom to redefine where and how we work. It encourages us to break free from the traditional office constraints and explore a world filled with possibilities. As remote workers, freelancers, and managers, we're at the forefront of a seismic shift in the workforce culture. This shift is one where geographical boundaries blur and diverse teams converge, creating a richer tapestry of perspectives and ideas.

For many, the transition to remote work has been a journey of self-discovery. It pushes us to understand not just our work tasks but also our personal needs and limitations. By mastering time management strategies and establishing firm boundaries, we've learned how to balance professional obligations with personal fulfillment. This balancing act enhances our productivity and ensures our well-being doesn't fall by the wayside.

The key to thriving in a remote environment lies in the seamless integration of technology and human connection. As we embrace digital communication tools, we must also nurture our interpersonal skills. Forming meaningful connections with colleagues across screens fosters a sense of belonging and unity. It's this connection that propels us forward, even as we sit miles apart.

At the core of this remote work evolution is the potential for personal growth and development. With unprecedented access to online learning resources, we're in an era where self-education is a powerful tool. Whether it's acquiring new skills or deepening existing ones, this endeavor is pivotal in staying competitive and fulfilled in our careers. All of us have the opportunity to become lifelong learners, continuously enriching our professional landscape.

Moreover, the rise of remote work has ushered in a new era of inclusivity in the workplace. It provides opportunities for those who might have been previously excluded due to traditional job constraints. Whether it's parents, individuals with disabilities, or those residing in remote locations, remote work levels the playing field, allowing everyone a chance to contribute effectively.

Nonetheless, the flexible nature of remote work also requires a heightened sense of responsibility and self-discipline. Complacency is easy when there's no one physically watching over us. Remote workers must cultivate an intrinsic drive to excel and innovate. This autonomy, when managed well, becomes a source of immense personal and professional satisfaction.

As we look to the future, the landscape of remote work will undoubtedly continue to evolve. Technological advancements and cultural shifts will shape how we work remotely. Yet, the fundamental principles of connection, adaptability, and innovation will remain constant. By staying attuned to these principles, you can navigate unforeseen changes with resilience and grace.

In conclusion, remote work is more than just a method of employment—it's a lifestyle choice that offers a pathway to a more balanced, fulfilling, and diverse professional experience. This guide has equipped you with the essential tools, strategies, and insights needed to thrive in this dynamic environment. As you venture forward, remember to embrace the journey, seize the opportunities, and continue to redefine the boundaries of what's possible in your remote work life.

# Appendix A: Appendix

As we conclude our exploration of the dynamic landscape of remote work, this appendix serves as a handy repository of supplementary information, references, and insights that can further enhance your journey. Though the preceding chapters have delved deeply into strategies, mindsets, and tools necessary for thriving in a decentralized work environment, this section offers additional context and resources to round out your understanding.

## Further Reading and Resources

Diving deeper into specific areas of remote work may require additional materials or resources. Whether it's about setting up the perfect home office or mastering communication tools, there's a wealth of literature, articles, and online courses available:

- For an exploration of creating effective remote workspaces, consider exploring books and articles that focus on ergonomics and design.
- Online platforms offer a multitude of courses on improving digital communication and leadership skills specific to virtual teams.
- Research journals and case studies that delve into trends and future predictions within remote work sectors can provide a broader industry perspective.

## Recommended Tools and Software

The consistent evolution of technology means that the tools available for remote work are constantly being updated and improved. Here are some suggestions to enhance your workflow:

1. **Project Management Software:** Applications like Trello or Asana offer platforms to manage tasks and timelines efficiently.
2. **Communication Tools:** Solutions such as Slack or Microsoft Teams facilitate seamless team interaction.
3. **Security and Privacy Solutions:** Invest in robust VPNs and encryption tools to safeguard your data.

## Community and Networking Opportunities

Building a supportive network is crucial for any remote worker. Engaging with online communities can provide both professional connections and personal support.

- Platforms like LinkedIn and industry-specific forums offer spaces to connect with fellow professionals and share insights.

- Participating in webinars and virtual conferences is a great way to stay informed and connected with the latest in your field.

This appendix wraps up the practical journey of thriving in remote work but also opens the door to continued exploration, learning, and growth. Keep adapting, exploring new tools, and connecting with your community. Remember, the world of remote work is as full of opportunities as it is challenges, and you're equipped to master both.

www.ingramcontent.com/pod-product-compliance
Lightning Source LLC
Chambersburg PA
CBHW071054240526
45471CB00015B/1869